GOOD HOUSEKEEPING

NEW · BASIC COOKERY

THE BEST INTRODUCTORY
BOOK FOR THE COOK

GOOD HOUSEKEEPING

NEW · BASIC COOKERY

THE BEST INTRODUCTORY
BOOK FOR THE COOK

Good Housekeeping Institute

Ebury Press London

Published by Ebury Press
National Magazine House
72 Broadwick Street
London W1V 2BP

First published 1966
Reprinted 1967
Reprinted 1969
Revised 1970
Reprinted 1972
Reprinted 1972
Revised Schools edition 1974
New Metricated edition 1976
Reprinted 1976
Completely Revised edition 1984

ISBN 0 85223 392 2

Designed by Graham Dudley
Illustrated by Bill le Fever

Filmset by Advanced Filmsetters (Glasgow) Ltd
Printed and bound by Hazell Watson and Viney Ltd, Aylesbury

CONTENTS

Introduction	
working from a recipe	6
using your oven	6
measuring	7
cooking equipment	8
glossary	10
Breakfasts	11
Soups and Starters	20
Fish	26
Meat	33
Poultry	55
Vegetables and Salads	59
Supper Dishes	71
Egg and Cheese Dishes	73
Rice and Pasta	79
Hot Puddings	85
Cold Puddings	91
Sauces, Stuffings and Accompaniments	98
Pastry	104
Cakes and Biscuits	107
Icing and Decorating	118
Breads and Scones	123
Index	126

INTRODUCTION

WORKING FROM A RECIPE

Before you start to make a dish, read the recipe right through and read also any general instructions at the beginning of the section or chapter. Next, collect together the cooking utensils you will need and do any preliminary preparation, such as greasing dishes, lining cake tins and so on. If the dish is to be baked, turn on the heat and set the thermostatic control so that the oven will be at the correct temperature when you are ready for it.

Finally, collect and measure out all the ingredients needed. If you are a beginner, it is sensible to follow the recipe exactly, scrupulously weighing and measuring the ingredients – leave variations for when you have more experience. Amounts of flavourings, seasonings and spices, sweetening, etc, may usually be varied to suit individual tastes, but basic ingredients like flour or fat should not be altered.

Follow closely the directions given in the recipe – seemingly slight changes in procedure may make all the difference between an outstanding dish and one that is only mediocre.

USING YOUR OVEN

1. Arrange the oven shelves before the oven is heated.

2. Set the thermostat to the required temperature 15–20 minutes before the food is to be put in. (Some dishes, such as milk puddings and casseroles, which require very long, slow cooking, can 'start from cold'.)

3. The centre of the oven corresponds most exactly to the dial setting; the upper part in some ovens is somewhat hotter, while the bottom of the oven is cooler.

4. Open the oven door as little as possible during the cooking time. With cakes in particular be very gentle, as an in-rush of cold air may spoil the baking.

5. When using the oven for browning au gratin dishes, etc, have it very hot and place the dishes at the top, otherwise the mixture will bubble without browning.

6. Put the pie dishes, casseroles, cake tins, etc, on baking sheets so that they are easier to move.

This table compares oven thermostats marked in °C with those marked in °F and with gas marks. These are dial markings and not exact conversions.

°C	°F	gas mark
290	550	
270	525	
250	500	
240	475	9
230	450	8
220	425	7
200	400	6
190	375	5
180	350	4
170	325	3
150	300	2
140	275	1
130	250	$\frac{1}{2}$
110	225	$\frac{1}{4}$
100	200	Low
80	175	
70	150	

MEASUR-ING

Use these equivalents to convert recipes from Imperial to metric measures or *vice versa*.

Imperial measurement	Approx. metric equivalent	Imperial measurement	Approx. metric equivalent
1 oz	25 g	9 oz	250 g
2 oz	50 g	10 oz	275 g
3 oz	75 g	11 oz	300 g
4 oz	100–125 g	12 oz	350 g
5 oz	150 g	13 oz	375 g
6 oz	175 g	14 oz	400 g
7 oz	200 g	15 oz	425 g
8 oz	225 g	16 oz (1 lb)	450 g

Imperial measurement	Approx. metric equivalent	Imperial measurement	Approx. metric equivalent
1 fl oz	25 ml	15 fl oz ($\frac{3}{4}$ pint)	450 ml
2 fl oz	50 ml	20 fl oz (1 pint)	600 ml
5 fl oz ($\frac{1}{4}$ pint)	150 ml	35 fl oz	1 litre
10 fl oz ($\frac{1}{2}$ pint)	300 ml		

QUICK HANDY MEASURES

Approximate equivalent shown in level 15-ml spoonfuls

Almonds, ground	$25 g = 3\frac{1}{2}$
Breadcrumbs, fresh	$25 g = 7$
Breadcrumbs, dried	$25 g = 3$
Butter, lard, etc	$25 g = 2$
Cheddar, grated	$25 g = 3$
Chocolate, grated	$25 g = 4$
Coffee, instant	$25 g = 6\frac{1}{2}$
Cornflour	$25 g = 2\frac{3}{4}$
Custard powder	$25 g = 2\frac{3}{4}$
Curry powder	$25 g = 4$
Flour, unsifted	$25 g = 3$
Suet, shredded	$25 g = 3$
Sugar, caster/gran.	$25 g = 2$
Sugar, demerara	$25 g = 2$
Sugar, icing	$25 g = 3$
Syrup or honey	$25 g = 1$

When following a recipe, choose either Imperial or metric measures and do not switch from one to the other. Use standard measuring spoons for small measures.

COOKING EQUIP-MENT

Excellent meals can be produced with surprisingly little equipment, but it does make the work easier if you have the right utensils and a few labour-saving devices that you can really use.
Make your own list of the basic items, using the notes below as a guide but bearing in mind your own circumstances. As storage space and cash allow you can then add other more expensive and specialised items which you would like. Avoid buying odd gadgets unless you are sure they will do a real job for you.
Choosing equipment can be tricky because of the wide variety on sale. However, Good Housekeeping Institute is constantly testing household goods and will be glad to advise you on buying an article which is suited to your purpose, well-designed, well-made and efficient. If you require information please send a stamped, addressed envelope to Good Housekeeping Institute, National Magazine House, 72 Broadwick St., London W1V 2BP.

Pots and pans
4 saucepans with lids in assorted sizes
1 milk saucepan, with non-stick finish, for sauces, etc
20.5-cm (8-inch) frying pan of fairly heavy quality (non-stick)
1 1.7-litre (3-pint) kettle

Kitchen china and ovenware
mixing bowl
2 pudding basins

2 casseroles, 1 large, 1 smaller
2 ovenproof plates
coffee pot or percolator

Baking tins
set of bun tins
18-cm (7-inch) cake tin
23-cm (9-inch) cake tin
two 18-cm (7-inch) sandwich tins, 2.5–4 cm
    (1–1½ inch) deep
Swiss roll tin
18-cm (7-inch) pie plate
baking sheet
wire cooling rack
roasting tin

General
kitchen scales
chopping board
rolling pin
pastry brush
grater with 2 or 3 sizes of hole
rotary egg whisk or electric whisk
lemon squeezer
colander
can opener
measuring jug (marked metric and Imperial)
measuring spoons
set of pastry cutters

Cutlery, spoons, tools
2 wooden spoons
2 forks
2 tablespoons
2 teaspoons
slotted spoon for draining
fish slice
skewers
mincer
apple corer/potato peeler
4 knives – 1 chopping, 1 vegetable, 1 bread and
    1 carving
carving fork
pair kitchen scissors
corkscrew/bottle opener

Storage equipment, etc
vegetable rack
storage jars and containers
bread bin
cake and biscuit tins
preserving jars
garbage bin

GLOSSARY

Bain Marie A vessel half-filled with just simmering water, used to keep sauces and soups hot without further cooking, or to prevent overheating of egg dishes baked in the oven.

Bake To cook in the oven by dry heat. Most cakes, pastries and breads are cooked this way, as well as some puddings and savoury dishes.

Baste To spoon over liquid (stock or fat) during cooking to prevent food drying out and to improve the appearance.

Beat To agitate an ingredient or mixture by vigorously turning it over and over with an upward motion, to incorporate air.

Bind To add a liquid, egg or melted fat to a dry mixture to hold it together.

Blanch To treat food with boiling water in order to whiten it, preserve its natural colour, loosen its skin, remove any strong or bitter taste or kill unwanted enzymes or bacteria before freezing or preserving.

Blend To mix flour, cornflour or similar with a cold liquid to form a smooth paste. A little hot liquid is then added, usually from the sauce, soup or stew to be thickened. This prevents lumps forming.

Boil To cook vegetables, rice, pasta etc in liquid heated to 100°C (212°F). Syrups and glazes that need to be reduced in quantity and thickened are also boiled.

Braise To bake or stew slowly on a bed of vegetables in a covered dish.

Consistency The term used to describe the texture of a cake or pudding mixture before it is cooked.

Pouring Consistency: The mixture should be soft enough to pour steadily from the bowl and find its own level.

Coating Consistency: The mixture should be thick enough to coat the back of a spoon.

Dropping Consistency: Fill a spoon with some of the mixture and hold it on its side above the bowl without jerking. The mixture should fall off reluctantly.

Cream To beat together fat and sugar to resemble whipped cream ie until pale and fluffy. This is used for cake and pudding mixtures.

Drain To remove surplus liquid or fat from foods by using a slotted spoon, colander, sieve or kitchen spoon.

Dice To cut up into small cubes.

Dredge, dust or flour To sprinkle food lightly with flour before frying or sugar to improve appearance.

Fold in To combine whisked or creamed mixtures with other ingredients so that it retains its lightness. This method is used for cake mixtures, soufflés and meringues and is done with a metal spoon, it cannot be successfully done in an electric food processor.

Fry To cook food in deep or shallow hot fat.

Glaze To give food a glossy surface before or after cooking. It improves flavour and appearance.

Grill To cook food in direct heat under a grill.

Knead To work a dough firmly using the heel of the hand for breadmaking, the fingertips in pastry making. In both cases the outside of the dough is drawn to the centre.

Poach To cook gently in liquid just below boiling point.

Purée To pass vegetables or fruit through a sieve to remove skins, fibres and pips and give a smooth, even texture. This can also be done in an electric blender or food processor.

Roast To cook meat or poultry in hot fat in the oven. Potatoes and vegetables may also be cooked in this way.

Roux A mixture of equal quantities of fat and flour cooked together for a few minutes. The mixture is used as a foundation for sauces.

Rubbing in A method of incorporating fat into flour, used in making shortcrust pastry, plain cakes and biscuits, when a short texture is required. The fat is cut into small pieces in the flour, then rubbed in with the fingertips.

Sauté To cook over a brisk heat in a fat such as butter or oil. The food must be tossed in the fat, either by shaking the pan or turning with a spatula so that it does not stick or burn.

Sieve To rub or press food through a sieve using a wooden spoon.

Sift To shake flour or similar through a sieve to aerate.

Simmer To keep a cooking liquid just below boiling point. The surface of the liquid should not bubble.

Steam To cook food in the steam from boiling water.

Stew To cook slowly and for a long time in an enclosed vessel.

Whisk or whip To beat air rapidly into a mixture either by hand using an egg beater, balloon whisk or electric mixer. It is continued until the food is quite stiff.

BREAKFASTS

Weekday breakfasts tend to become a hurried, skimped affair of a piece of toast and a quick cup of tea – the old-fashioned hearty breakfast is now a weekend or holiday treat. However, it is important to start the day with an adequate even if light meal. Many people find cereal or fruit, followed by toast and marmalade, are quite sufficient, but some families require a more substantial breakfast with something cooked.

Any cooked dish for breakfast use needs to be quickly prepared, so frying and grilling are the most popular methods to use. To save time in the morning, it is a good plan to lay the table the night before and to leave ready everything that will be needed for the meal.

BREAK-FAST FRUITS

Almost any fresh or stewed fruit is suitable for eating at breakfast, either alone or mixed with cereals; it is usually served simply in individual dishes. If necessary, fresh fruit may be prepared overnight, though as this results in loss of the valuable vitamin C, it should not be done as a general rule.

Fruit juices are another popular breakfast item; prepare your own fresh juice if you wish, but cartoned, bottled, canned or frozen products are easier and cheaper to use and nutritionally just as sound. Serve them either neat or diluted with water. The most usual breakfast juices are unsweetened grapefruit, orange, pineapple and tomato juices, but the juice of other fruits, such as blackcurrants or raspberries, may be served when in season.

> To obtain the juice from soft fruit, simmer it gently with a little water until tender; strain or sieve and sweeten if necessary.

ORANGES

Peel the oranges, removing as much as possible of the white pith, then slice fairly thinly across the segments. Flick out any pips with the point of a knife. Sprinkle with sugar if you wish.

GRAPEFRUIT

Cut the fruit in half and cut round each half with a curved grapefruit knife, loosening the flesh from the outer skin. Cut between the segments to loosen the flesh from the membranes, remove the centre core and pips. Sprinkle with sugar if you wish.

Preparing the grapefruit

CEREALS

PREPARED CEREALS

There are many popular ready-to serve cereals on the market, which require no preparation at all. They may be served with hot or cold milk and sugar if not already sweetened, or with fruit – fresh, canned or stewed.

APPLE MUESLI

Serves 4

60 ml (4 level tbsp) rolled oats or fine oatmeal
150 ml ($\frac{1}{4}$ pint) fruit juice
4 eating apples
60 ml (4 tbsp) cream or top of the milk

15 ml (1 tbsp) honey
a little brown sugar
50 g (2 oz) sultanas or raisins
a few chopped nuts (walnuts, almonds, etc.)

Place the oats and fruit juice in a bowl and leave overnight ■ The next day grate the apples (with their skins on); keep a little back for decoration and mix the rest with the remaining ingredients (except the nuts) ■ Put into glasses, top with some grated apple and sprinkle with chopped nuts.

YOGURT WITH DRIED FRUIT

Serves 4

450 g (1 lb) dried fruit (see below)
100–175 g (4–6 oz) Demerara sugar

piece of lemon rind
plain yogurt to serve

Choose from the wide range of dried fruits – apricots, prunes, figs, pears, apples or peaches. Serve just one fruit or make a dried fruit salad. Wash the fruit and soak it for several hours (or overnight) in 600 ml (1 pint) water. Cook them in this water, adding the sugar and lemon rind. Stew gently till tender and serve cold with plain yogurt.

PORRIDGE

Serves 2–3

600 ml (1 pint) water   salt to taste
50 g (2 oz) rolled oats

Heat the water and when it is boiling sprinkle in the oats, stirring vigorously with a wooden spoon. Continue to stir and boil for about 5 minutes, then add salt to taste; serve very hot.

EGGS

Breakfast cookery is easy with eggs; they can be quickly cooked in a variety of ways.
Hens' eggs are generally used for breakfast dishes, but fresh duck, turkey or goose eggs may be used if available. Turkey and goose eggs are large, so allow about 7 minutes for boiling. Duck eggs must be cooked very thoroughly, not soft-boiled.

HOW TO BREAK AN EGG

Hold the egg over the saucepan or a bowl, and either gently tap it on the side of the pan or bowl, or give it a gentle tap with a knife to break the shell. Put your thumbs on each side of the crack and pull the shell apart ■ To separate the yolk from the white, tip the yolk carefully from one half of the shell to the other, until all the white has slid into the bowl below.

BOILED EGGS

1–2 eggs per person

Lower the eggs gently into a pan of boiling water, using a spoon. Lower the heat and cook for $3\frac{1}{2}$ minutes for a light set, and up to 5 minutes for a firmer set ■ Alternatively, put them in cold water and bring slowly to the boil – then cook for 3–4 minutes ■ Fresh eggs take a little longer to cook than those which are a few days old.

POACHED EGGS

1–2 eggs per person   salt and pepper
butter   buttered toast to serve

Simmer some water gently in the lower pan of the poacher and melt a small knob of butter in each cup ■ Break the eggs one at a time and put into the cups; season lightly, cover and simmer gently for 3–4 minutes, or until lightly set ■ Serve on hot buttered toast ■ To poach eggs in a frying pan, half fill it with water and add a pinch of salt or a few drops of vinegar ■ Bring the water to the boil and slip the eggs into the water. Cook gently until lightly set and lift out with a slotted spoon or fish slice ■ Drain the eggs before serving as above.

Melting butter in each cup

FRIED EGGS

lard, oil or dripping   1–2 eggs per person

Heat the fat in a frying pan. Break each egg into a cup, drop carefully into the hot fat and cook gently until set, basting with hot fat so that the eggs are cooked on top ■ Remove from the pan with a fish slice or spatula.

SCRAMBLED EGGS

Serves 2

25 g (1 oz) butter or   60 ml (4 tbsp) milk
   margarine   salt and pepper
4 eggs   buttered toast to serve

Melt the butter or margarine slowly in a saucepan ■ Break 4 eggs one at a time into a basin, add the milk and some seasoning ■ Pour the egg mixture into the pan, cook slowly over gentle heat, stirring all the time until the mixture is creamy ■ Serve on hot buttered toast.

Mixing egg and milk

SAUSAGES

Both pork and beef sausages may be used for break-fast, either grilled or fried; they can be served with fried bread, tomatoes or mushrooms. Sausagemeat may be made into flat cakes, which are fried or baked.

FRIED SAUSAGES

Serves 4

450 g (1 lb) pork or beef   25 g (1 oz) fat
   sausages

Heat the fat in a frying pan, then add the sausages carefully and cook them gently, browning them evenly ■ It is important to cook slowly, so that the skins do not split and so that the insides are thoroughly done. Allow about 15–20 minutes, accord-ing to size.

GRILLED SAUSAGES

Serves 4

450 g (1 lb) pork or beef
   sausages

Cook under a fairly hot grill, turning frequently until evenly browned and cooked through; allow about 15–20 minutes.

BACON

Bacon, either fried or grilled, and served with a fried egg and fried bread, is probably the favourite English breakfast dish.

> When buying bacon remember that the fat should be firm and white and the lean a deep pink. Back, streaky, collar or gammon rashers are all suitable for both frying and grilling. Bacon is usually sliced rather thinly, but gammon is generally preferred cut a little thicker.

To prepare bacon for cooking, cut off the rind and remove any bones with kitchen scissors. To make sure that the rashers will be quite flat when cooked, snip through the fat at intervals. If on the other hand you like a wavy effect in the cooked rashers, smooth them with the flat of a knife. Unless the bacon is very lean, no extra fat is needed.

To grill bacon, lay the rashers on the grill rack with the fat parts over the lean. Place under a hot grill, turning it once. Lean rashers should be brushed with fat or oil before cooking. Cook quickly for crisp bacon, slowly if you prefer the rashers softer.

FRIED BACON

bacon rashers – allow
1–2 per person

Lay streaky or back rasher in a cold pan, with the lean parts over the fat. Cook very gently, especially at first while the fat is melting ■ Turn once during cooking.

GRILLED BACON

bacon rashers   *fat or oil*

Lay the rashers on the grill rack with the fat parts over the lean. Place under a hot grill, turning it once ■ Lean rashers should be brushed with fat or oil before cooking ■ Cook quickly for crisp bacon, slowly if you prefer the rashers softer.

FRIED BREAD

For this traditional accompaniment to the cooked British breakfast, heat some fat in a frying pan and fry the slices of bread until crisp on both sides.

KIPPERS

Kippered herrings may be purchased boned or un-boned, wrapped or unwrapped, frozen or fresh. When serving whole kippers, allow 1–2 per person, according to size. Prepare by washing in cold water, then cutting off the heads, small fins and tail, using kitchen scissors.

POACHED KIPPERS

1–2 whole kippers or   *butter*
  3–4 fillets per person

Put the fish into a frying pan, cover with boiling water and poach gently for about 5 minutes or until tender. Drain and serve with a knob of butter on each kipper.

Covering the kippers with water

> To reduce the rather unpleasant smell from kippers, they may be cooked in a covered dish: pour on boiling water and cover closely with a lid or plate. Leave for 5–10 minutes, pour off the water and serve with a knob of butter.

GRILLED KIPPERS

1–2 whole kippers or   *butter*
  3–4 fillets per person

Dot the kippers with butter and grill gently for 4–5 minutes on each side.

BAKED KIPPERS

1–2 whole kippers or   *butter*
  3–4 fillets per person

Wrap the kippers in foil and place in the oven at 190°C (375°F) mark 5. Serve with a knob of butter.

KIDNEYS

Sheep's, calf's and pig's kidneys have a better flavour and are much more acceptable for breakfast dishes than ox kidney, which is more suitable for pies or stews. Kidneys served with bacon make a good substantial breakfast. Allow $1\frac{1}{2}$–2 kidneys per person. For Grilled Kidneys see recipe on page 54. For Fried Kidneys, prepare as for Grilled Kidneys but dip the Kidneys in a little seasoned flour and fry in hot fat for 10 minutes.

COFFEE

COFFEE

There are many different types of coffee available each with its distinctive flavour. It is worth trying a few separately and in a blend until you find the ones you like ■ There are also different grades of roasted beans, the degree of roasting affecting the flavour of the coffee, dark beans (high-roasted) giving a stronger flavour ■ You can buy roasted beans and grind them yourself, or you can buy vacuum-packed ready-ground coffee. It is essential to choose the correct grind for your method of making coffee.

Good coffee may be made in several ways and it is not essential to have special equipment. Whichever method is followed, however, you must use fresh coffee and sufficient of it. For breakfast it is usual to serve coffee with hot milk – generally 1 part milk to 2 parts coffee. The milk should be hot, but never boiled, and is served in a separate heated jug. Black coffee is usually made quite strong.

All the equipment must be kept scrupulously clean or the coffee will be unsatisfactory. If it is necessary to reheat coffee, do not let it boil.

Making coffee in an earthenware jug

Find out the approximate capacity of your jug so that you can judge the amount of water in it. Warm the jug, then put in 40–50 g (1½–2 oz) medium-ground coffee per 600 ml (1 pint) water. Pour on fast-boiling water, stir vigorously, cover and keep in a warm place to infuse for 4–5 minutes. Strain the coffee into a warmed coffee pot or straight into the cups.

Straining the coffee into pot

Making coffee in a saucepan

Put the measured water in a saucepan with 40–50 g (1½–2 oz) medium or coarsely-ground coffee per 600 ml (1 pint) and place over the heat. Stir well and bring almost to boiling point. Remove the pan from the heat, stir, cover the pan and leave in a warm place or over a very low heat for about 5 minutes. Strain the coffee into a heated jug.

Instant coffee

This provides a very quick, easy way of making coffee. Allow 5 ml (1 level tsp) instant coffee powder or granules per cup. Fill the cups three-quarters full with boiling water and top up with warm or cold milk, if liked.

Making coffee in a percolator

Place 40–50 g (1½–2 oz) medium or coarsely-ground coffee per 600 ml (1 pint) water in the perforated basket and put the water in the base. Bring the water to the boil, lower the heat and allow the water to percolate through the coffee for 8–10 minutes. Remove coffee basket and serve at once. Electric models automatically switch off after a pre-set time and then keep the coffee warm.

Placing coffee in basket

Making coffee in a cona or syphon machine

Place the water in the lower bowl and put on to heat. Place the filter in the neck of the upper bowl and put in 40–50 g (1½–2 oz) medium-ground coffee per 600 ml (1 pint) water. When the water in the lower bowl boils, fit the upper bowl on top. Allow the water to rise to the upper bowl. Leave to infuse for 2–3 minutes, then draw the machine from the heat and allow the water to run back into the lower bowl.

Placing coffee in upper bowl

Filter coffee

Place a filter paper in the filter attachment and put in 75 ml (4½ level tbsp) finely-ground coffee per 600 ml (1 pint) water. Place the filter over a heated jug and pour boiling water slowly over the coffee grounds, allowing it to filter through. Electric coffee filters boil the water, syphon it over the grounds and keep the coffee hot for you.

Placing coffee in filter

TEA

Buy tea in small quantities and keep it in an airtight tin or jar so that the aroma and strength are conserved.

The usual amount to allow is 5 ml (1 level tsp) per person; when making tea for more than three people, it is usual to allow 5 ml (1 level tsp) per person and 5 ml (1 level tsp) 'for the pot'. Use freshly boiled water.

Warm the pot, put in the measured quantity of tea, pour on the boiling water and leave to infuse before pouring out. The time required for infusion depends on the type of tea used; Indian teas usually require 4–5 minutes, but China teas infuse more quickly and can be poured out 2–3 minutes after being made.

When using teabags allow 1 bag per person (don't add an extra one 'for the pot').

Indian teas are usually taken with milk, with or without sugar to taste, but some people prefer sliced lemon to milk. China teas are always served with lemon slices, not milk.

Pouring on the boiling water

SOUPS AND STARTERS

STOCKS

Good full-bodied stock is the foundation of great soups and casseroles. When possible make your own, but there are numerous ready-made stock preparations – the most popular being stock cubes – which save much time and trouble. Don't forget that these are well seasoned and inclined to be salty – so do not add extra seasoning until after checking the flavour at the final stage. If you have a freezer, keep stock frozen for up to 3 months as a useful standby.

BASIC MEAT STOCK

Makes about 1.1 litres (2 pints)

900 g (2 lb) meat bones, fresh or from cooked meat
cold water
2 onions, skinned and roughly chopped
2 sticks celery, scrubbed and roughly chopped
2 carrots, peeled and roughly chopped
5 ml (1 level tsp) salt
3 peppercorns
bouquet garni

Wash the bones and chop them up. Put them in a large saucepan and add 2 litres ($3\frac{1}{2}$ pints) water; bring to the boil and skim off any scum ■ Add the roughly chopped vegetables, salt, peppercorns and bouquet garni and simmer, tightly covered, for 5–6 hours ■ If you have a pressure cooker, use only 1.4 litres ($2\frac{1}{2}$ pints) water, bring to high pressure and cook for 1–$1\frac{1}{4}$ hours. Reduce pressure at room temperature ■ When cooked, strain the stock and leave to go cold. Chill and remove all traces of fat.

CHICKEN STOCK

Makes about 1.1 litres (2 pints)

roast chicken carcass
flavouring vegetables (onions, carrots, celery)
herbs
1.4–1.7 litres ($2\frac{1}{2}$–3 pints) water

Break down the carcass and bones of a carved roast chicken and include any skin, chicken scraps, etc. Add the water and bring to the boil ■ Skim off any scum that rises and add flavouring vegetables and herbs if you wish. Cover tightly and simmer for 3 hours ■ If you have a pressure cooker, use only 1.1 litres (2 pints) water, bring to high pressure and cook for 45–60 minutes. Reduce pressure at room temperature ■ When cooked, strain the stock and leave to go cold. Chill and remove all traces of fat.

FRENCH ONION SOUP

Serves 4

40 g (1½ oz) butter or margarine
225 g (8 oz) onions, skinned and chopped
15 ml (1 level tbsp) plain flour

900 ml (1½ pints) beef stock
salt and pepper
a bay leaf
4 slices of French bread grated cheese

Melt the butter and fry the onions until they are well and evenly browned, taking care not to let the pieces become too dark. Add the flour and mix well ▪ Pour on the boiling stock, add some salt and pepper and the bay leaf and simmer for 30 minutes; remove the bay leaf ▪ Put the slices of French bread in a soup tureen, pour on the soup and top with grated cheese ▪ Alternatively, pour the soup into a fireproof casserole, float the slices of bread on it and cover with the grated cheese; then brown under the grill for a few minutes.

Adding the flour

TOMATO SOUP

Serves 4

25 g (1 oz) butter or margarine
1 stick of celery, washed and chopped
1 small onion, skinned and finely chopped
1 carrot, peeled and sliced
1 rasher of bacon, rinded and chopped
30 ml (2 level tbsp) plain flour

a bouquet garni
700 g (1½ lb) tomatoes, quartered
600 ml (1 pint) chicken stock
salt and pepper
a little sugar
lemon juice

Melt the butter and cook the celery, onion, carrot and bacon for 5 minutes. Sprinkle in the flour and stir well ▪ Add the bouquet garni, tomatoes, stock and seasoning. Cover and cook gently for 30 minutes ▪ Rub the soup through a sieve or purée it in a blender then sieve to remove the seeds and any small pieces of skin. Return it to the pan, check the seasoning, add a little sugar and lemon juice and reheat.

CREAM OF MUSHROOM SOUP

Serves 4

225 g (8 oz) mushrooms, sliced
1 small onion, skinned and sliced
300 ml ($\frac{1}{2}$ pint) chicken stock
25 g (1 oz) butter or margarine

45 ml (3 level tbsp) plain flour
450 ml ($\frac{3}{4}$ pint) milk
salt and pepper
45 ml (3 tbsp) cream

Cook the mushrooms and onion in the stock, covered, for about 30 minutes. Let them cool slightly then purée in a blender or rub through a sieve ▪ Melt the butter, stir in the flour and cook for 2–3 minutes. Remove the pan from the heat and gradually stir in the milk; bring to the boil and continue to stir until it thickens ▪ Add the mushroom purée, season with salt and pepper and simmer for 15 minutes. Allow to cool slightly and stir in the cream ▪ Reheat without boiling and, if you wish, garnish with lightly fried sliced mushrooms.

Soup is often served accompanied by croutons, little pieces of bread which are fried or toasted, and sprinkled over the soup.

MINESTRONE

Serves 4

$\frac{1}{2}$ leek, shredded and washed
1 onion, skinned and finely chopped
1 garlic clove, skinned and crushed
25 g (1 oz) butter or margarine
1 litre (1$\frac{3}{4}$ pints) beef stock
1 carrot, peeled and cut in thin strips
1 turnip, peeled and cut in thin strips
1 stick of celery, trimmed and thinly sliced

45 ml (3 level tbsp) shortcut macaroni
$\frac{1}{4}$ cabbage, washed and finely shredded
3 runner beans, thinly sliced
45 ml (3 tbsp) fresh or frozen peas
5 ml (1 level tsp) tomato purée or 4 tomatoes, skinned and diced
1–2 rashers of bacon, rinded, chopped and fried
salt and pepper
grated Parmesan cheese

Lightly fry the leek, onion and garlic in the melted butter for 5–10 minutes, until soft ▪ Add the stock, bring to the boil, add the carrot, turnip, celery and macaroni and simmer, covered, for 20–30 minutes ▪ Add the cabbage, beans and peas, cover and simmer for a further 20 minutes ▪ Stir in the tomato purée or tomatoes, bacon and seasoning to taste. Bring back to the boil. Serve the grated Parmesan cheese in a separate dish.

Rinding bacon

WATERCRESS SOUP

Serves 4

2 bunches watercress
50 g (2 oz) butter or
   margarine
1 onion, skinned and
   chopped

25 g (1 oz) plain flour
750 ml (1¼ pints) chicken
   stock
300 ml (½ pint) milk
salt and pepper

Wash the watercress and reserve a few sprigs to garnish. Cut away any coarse stalks. Chop the leaves and remaining stalks ▪ Melt the butter in a pan and stir in the watercress and onion. Cook over a gentle heat for about 15 minutes until soft. Stir in the flour stock, milk and seasoning. Bring to the boil, stirring continuously. Simmer gently for 30 minutes ▪ Cool slightly, then purée in a blender or rub through a sieve ▪ Return the soup to the pan and reheat. Garnish with watercress sprigs.

CHICKEN SOUP

Serves 4

25 g (1 oz) butter or
   margarine
1 medium onion, skinned
   and finely chopped
30 ml (2 level tbsp) plain
   flour
600 ml (1 pint) chicken
   stock
about 100 g (4 oz) cold
   cooked chicken

300 ml (½ pint) milk
1.25 ml (¼ level tsp)
   ground nutmeg
1.25 ml (¼ level tsp) dried
   thyme
salt and pepper
45 ml (3 tbsp) single
   cream
chopped fresh parsley to
   serve

Melt the butter in a large saucepan and fry the onion gently for 5 minutes until soft ▪ Stir in the flour then, stirring all the time, add the chicken stock, chicken, milk, nutmeg, thyme and salt and pepper to taste. Bring to the boil then cover and simmer gently for 5 minutes ▪ Stir in the cream and serve sprinkled with chopped parsley.

CHICKEN LIVER PÂTÉ

Serves 8

700 g (1½ lb) chicken
   livers
75 g (3 oz) butter
1 medium onion, skinned
   and finely chopped
1 large garlic clove,
   skinned and crushed

15 ml (1 tbsp) double
   cream
30 ml (2 level tbsp)
   tomato purée
45 ml (3 tbsp) sherry or
   brandy
melted butter (optional)

Rinse the chicken livers and dry thoroughly on absorbent kitchen paper ▪ Fry them in the butter until they change colour. Reduce the heat, add the onion and garlic, cover and cook for 5 minutes. Remove from the heat and cool ▪ Add the cream, tomato purée and sherry or brandy. Purée in a blender or press through a sieve ▪ Turn into 8 individual dishes and cover the tops with melted butter if you wish. Chill.

MACKEREL PÂTÉ

Serves 4

350 g (12 oz) smoked
  mackerel fillets
50 g (2 oz) butter,
  softened
60 ml (4 level tbsp)
  mayonnaise
5 ml (1 level tsp) snipped
  fresh chives

freshly ground pepper
grated rind and juice of
  ½ a lemon
parsley sprigs and lemon
  slices to garnish
fingers of hot toast to
  serve

Remove the skin and any bones from the mackerel fillets ■ Place the flesh in a bowl and add the butter, mayonnaise, chives, pepper, lemon rind and juice. Mix well together ■ Divide the pâté equally between 4 individual dishes and garnish with parsley and lemon slices ■ Serve with fingers of hot toast.

Removing skin

DRESSED AVOCADOS

Removing stone

avocados (allow half per
  person)
lemon juice
French dressing (see
  page 68), or shelled
  shrimps or prawns plus

thin mayonnaise (see
  page 68) or soured
  cream and seasoning
lettuce leaves (optional)

Cut open the avocados lengthwise, using a stainless steel knife and making a deep cut through the flesh, up to the stone and entirely encircling the fruit ■ Separate the halves by gently rotating them in opposite directions and discard the stone. Brush the cut surfaces with lemon juice ■ Serve with French dressing spooned into the hollow of each avocado half, or fill the hollow with shelled shrimps or prawns moistened with thin mayonnaise or well seasoned soured cream. If you wish serve the avocados on lettuce leaves.

CORN ON THE COB

corn cobs (allow 1–2 per
  person)

salt and pepper
melted butter

Remove the sheath and silky threads from the corn ■ Cook in boiling unsalted water for 12–20 minutes, or until the kernels are soft ■ Sprinkle with salt and pepper and serve with melted butter; put a cocktail stick in each end of the cobs to make them easier to eat.

Removing sheath and threads

Salt added to the water will toughen the corn, so do not add it until serving.

FLORIDA COCKTAIL

Serves 4

2 small grapefruit
2 large oranges
sugar

curaçao or any orange liqueur (optional)

Working over a plate, prepare the grapefruit as follows: remove all the skin, peeling the fruit with a sawing action and cutting deep enough to show the pulp ■ Holding the fruit in one hand, remove the flesh of each segment by cutting down at the side of the membrane and then scraping the segment off the membrane on the opposite side on to the plate ■ Repeat the process for the oranges. Mix the segments, together with any juice collected on the plate. Add curaçao if you wish and sugar, to taste ■ Divide the fruit between 4 glasses and pour a little juice into each. Serve chilled.

BLUE CHEESE DIP

100 g (4 oz) Danish Blue or Roquefort cheese, softened
75 g (3 oz) full fat soft cheese, softened

15 ml (1 tbsp) lemon juice
salt

Blend all the ingredients to a smooth cream with salt to taste and serve with chunks of French bread or vegetable dunks such as carrot sticks, radishes, celery curls, cucumber sticks.

FISH

TYPES OF FISH

Many fish are available frozen. Use like fresh fish but follow any instructions on the pack concerning storage, thawing and cooking.

There are many types of fish sold, but those described here tend to be the most popular in Great Britain.

Cod   A large, white-fleshed fish, which can be bought as fillets, steaks and cutlets. Cod can be grilled, fried or baked or used in made-up dishes. As its taste is not strong, it needs careful seasoning and flavouring.

Coley (Saithe, Coalfish)   A round fish with almost black skin and greyish flesh which turns white on cooking. Use in the same ways as cod or haddock.

Haddock   Another large, white-fleshed fish, with a good flavour. Haddock can be bought as fillets, steaks and cutlets and cooked by most methods.

Finnan haddock   Fairly small haddock, split open and lightly brined, then smoked on the bone. It has an excellent flavour and is traditionally served poached or grilled. When cooked and flaked, it can be used in made-up dishes such as kedgeree.
Golden fillets (or cutlets) have the backbone removed before they are smoked.
Smoked haddock or cod fillets are generally taken from larger fish and may therefore be coarse-textured.

Hake   Similar to cod, but with firmer white flesh. It can be cooked by any method suitable for cod.

Halibut   A large flat fish, usually sold in slices or steaks. It has white flesh and a delicate flavour and is one of the more expensive kinds of fish. It is usually grilled, baked or poached.

FISH

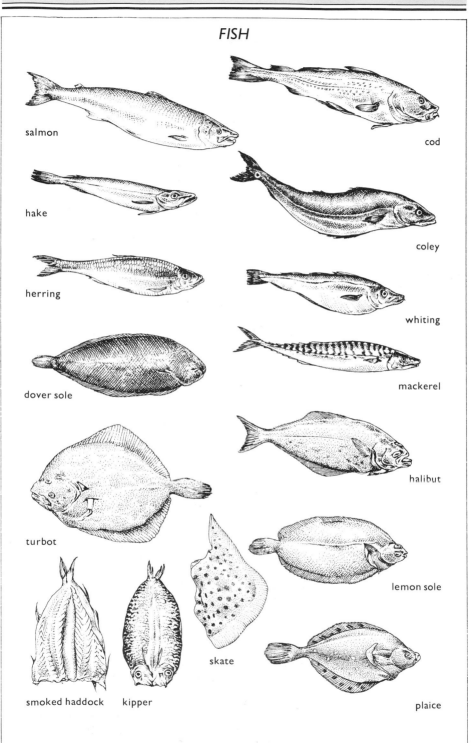

salmon

cod

hake

coley

herring

whiting

dover sole

mackerel

turbot

halibut

lemon sole

smoked haddock   kipper

skate

plaice

Herring A fairly small, round-bodied fish with a silvery skin and creamy-fawn oily flesh. It has a distinctive flavour. Herrings are cheap and are usually sold whole but the fishmonger will fillet them on request. They are suitable for grilling, frying, baking and sousing.

Kipper These are herrings split open, brined and smoked on the bone. Good kippers have an excellent flavour and can be poached, grilled or baked.

Mackerel A round-bodied oily fish, slightly larger than the herring; it has a characteristic green and black marbling on the skin. The creamy-coloured flesh has a distinctive flavour. It is sold whole or filleted. The flesh of mackerel is close-textured and the fish can be grilled, fried, baked or soused.

Plaice A flat fish with a dark grey top skin dotted with characteristic closely-set orange-red spots. The flesh is white, with a very delicate flavour. Plaice is usually sold filleted; it is cooked by grilling, frying, steaming and baking.

Salmon A large fish with silvery skin and a deep orange-red flesh that has a firm, close texture and distinctive flavour. Salmon is a very expensive fish; it is sold in steaks and as tail end and middle cut pieces; when small, the fish are sold whole. It is suitable for poaching, grilling and baking and can be served either hot or cold.

Skate A flat fish with slightly pink flesh and a moist, shiny skin. Only the 'wings' or side parts of the fish are sold. Fry or poach.

Dover sole One of the finest flat fish, more oval in shape than plaice, with a darkish brown-grey skin. Its flesh is firm and delicate with a delicious flavour. An expensive fish, it is sold whole or as fillets. Can be cooked by most methods, and is the basis of many classic fish dishes.

Lemon sole (*Witch sole*) Similar to Dover sole but the flesh is coarser and the flavour is not so fine. Cook as for plaice.

Turbot A very large flat fish usually sold in thick slices or cutlets. It is a delicious and expensive fish, but its white flesh is firm in texture, so a large amount is not required. It can be poached, baked or grilled.

Whiting A round-bodied fish with fine textured, delicately flavoured flesh. Cook whole or in fillets, by any of the usual methods.

FRIED PLAICE FILLETS

Serves 2

4 fillets of plaice or sole
seasoned flour
1 egg, beaten

dry white breadcrumbs
50 g (2 oz) butter or lard
lemon wedges

Wipe the fillets and dip in seasoned flour, shaking off any excess. Dip the fillets in beaten egg then coat in breadcrumbs, making sure that the coating is firm ■ Fry the fillets in the hot butter or lard for 3–5 minutes; turn them and fry for a further 2–3 minutes until crisp and golden brown ■ Drain on absorbent kitchen paper and serve garnished with lemon wedges.

Coating with breadcrumbs

SEASONED FLOUR

Mix about 30 ml (2 level tbsp) flour with about 5 ml (1 level tsp) salt and a good sprinkling of pepper ■ This is used for dusting meat or fish before frying or stewing. Either pat it on to the meat or fish, or dip pieces in the flour and shake them gently before cooking.

BAKED PLAICE WITH MUSHROOMS

Serves 4

8 fillets of plaice
a squeeze of lemon juice
salt and pepper
50 g (2 oz) mushrooms, sliced
1 small onion, skinned and finely chopped

45 ml (3 tbsp) milk
15 ml (1 level tbsp) cornflour
sprigs of parsley

Grease an ovenproof dish. Fold each fillet with both ends underneath and place in the dish; squeeze some lemon juice over and season with salt and pepper ■ Sprinkle the mushrooms and onion on top and add the milk. Bake in the oven at 190°C (375°F) mark 5 for 15–20 minutes. Transfer the fillets to a serving dish ■ Blend the cornflour with the remaining fish liquor and put in a saucepan; bring to the boil and cook for 1 minute. Pour this sauce over the fillets and garnish with parsley.

FISH IN BATTER

Serves 4

oil for deep frying
4 pieces of cod fillet
   (or other fish)
seasoned flour

1 egg
125 g (4 oz) plain flour
150 ml (¼ pint) milk
lemon wedges

Heat the oil slowly in a deep saucepan or deep fat fryer to 177°–188°C (350°–370°F). Wipe the fish and toss in seasoned flour ■ Mix together the egg, flour and half the milk, beat until smooth, then gradually add the rest of the milk, beating all the time ■ Coat the fish with the batter and gently lower it into the fat with a slotted spoon or fish slice. Fry until golden brown, then drain on absorbent kitchen paper. Serve with lemon wedges.

Coating fish with flour   Coating fish with batter

If a thermometer is not being used to check the correct temperature for frying, put in a 2.5-cm (1-inch) cube of bread, which should brown in 60 seconds.

GRILLED MACKEREL

Serves 4

4 mackerel   oil

Wash the mackerel, scrape off the scales and cut off the heads and tails. Slit the underside of the fish and remove the entrails, then wash and dry the fish ■ Make large slashes at 3 cm (1¼ inch) intervals and brush with oil ■ Place the mackerel on the grid of the grill-pan and cook under a hot grill for 5–8 minutes each side, depending on thickness.

Slashing mackerel

HERRINGS IN OATMEAL

Serves 4

4 herrings, cleaned and
  filleted
salt and pepper

fine oatmeal
50 g (2 oz) lard or butter

Wipe the herrings. Season and coat them with the oatmeal and fry in hot lard or butter until golden brown, turning them once to ensure that they are evenly cooked – about 6–8 minutes. Drain well on absorbent kitchen paper.

POACHED SMOKED HADDOCK

Serves 4

350–450 g (¾–1 lb)
  smoked haddock

butter to serve

Wash the fish and cut off the tail and any fins; if it is large, cut into pieces. Place in a pan, just cover with a little milk and water and cook very gently for 10–15 minutes. Drain and serve with a knob of butter.

FISH PIE

Serves 4

450 g (1 lb) haddock
  fillets
450 g (1 lb) potatoes,
  peeled
salt
50 g (2 oz) butter or
  margarine
½ onion, skinned and chopped

50 g (2 oz) streaky bacon,
  rinded and chopped
30 ml (2 level tbsp) plain
  flour
226-g (8-oz) can tomatoes
pepper
30–45 ml (2–3 tbsp) milk

Cut the haddock into 5-cm (2-inch) pieces. Put the potatoes in a saucepan, cover with water, add 5 ml (1 level tsp) salt and bring to the boil; simmer for 20–30 minutes until tender ■ Meanwhile, melt the butter or margarine in a shallow pan and fry the onion gently for 10 minutes – do not let it colour. Add the bacon and fish and cook for a further 5 minutes. Add the flour and blend well, then stir in the tomatoes. Bring to the boil, season and pour into a casserole. ■ Drain the potatoes and mash with a little milk and seasoning till smooth. Pile the potatoes on top of the fish, level the surface with a knife and mark with a fork. Bake in the oven at 200°C (400°F) mark 6 for 30 minutes, until the top is golden brown.

Cutting haddock into pieces

Piling potatoes on fish

KEDGEREE

Serves 4

350 g (12 oz) cooked
    smoked haddock or
    golden cutlet
2 eggs, hard-boiled
75 g (3 oz) butter or
    margarine

125 g (4 oz) long grain
    rice, cooked
salt and pepper
chopped fresh parsley

Flaking fish with fork

Remove the skin and bone from the haddock and flake the fish with a fork. Chop one of the hard-boiled eggs and mix with the fish ▪ Melt the butter in a saucepan and add the rice, fish and egg mixture and seasoning to taste ▪ Stir thoroughly over the heat until the kedgeree is heated through, pile it into a serving dish and garnish with chopped parsley and the remaining egg, cut into neat slices.

CHEESY GRILLED COD

Serves 4

4 cod cutlets, weighing
    about 700 g (1½ lb)
100 g (4 oz) Cheddar
    cheese, grated
½ small onion, skinned and
    grated

50 g (2 oz) butter or
    margarine, softened
2.5 ml (½ level tsp)
    mustard powder
salt and pepper
1 tomato, sliced

Wash and trim the cutlets. Put the cheese, onion, butter, mustard and seasoning in a bowl, and mix well together ▪ Place the cod steaks on the grill rack and grill under a medium heat for about 5 minutes, turn them and grill for a further 3 minutes ▪ Spread the cheese mixture over the fish and grill for 2–3 minutes until golden brown and bubbling. Place a slice of tomato on each cutlet, heat quickly and serve at once.

MEAT

The price of meat varies according to the type of cut, the lean tender parts usually being the most expensive. These cuts can be roasted, fried or grilled, while the tougher parts need slower cooking methods to soften them. The cheaper cuts are just as nutritious as the dearer ones and have just as good a flavour if cooked appropriately.

BEEF

HOW TO CHOOSE BEEF

Lean beef should be bright red, the fat creamy to yellow ■ There should be small flecks of fat through the lean; this fat (called 'marbling') helps to keep the lean moist and tender when the meat is cooking ■ Avoid meat with a line of gristle between lean and fat, which usually suggests it has come from an old animal.

CUTS AND METHODS OF COOKING

Sirloin A large joint from the loin end of the ribs, usually sold on the bone, but it can also be boned and rolled. It is roasted or cut into steaks (see below). With bone, allow 225–350 g (8–12 oz) per person. Without bone, allow 175–225 g (6–8 oz) per person.

Rib A fairly large joint, next to the sirloin; it can be bought on the bone or boned and rolled, and is roasted. Can also be used for pot roasting, braising and boiling. Quantities as for sirloin.

Topside A lean joint, containing no bone, which is therefore economical. It can be roasted in a slow oven, but is often braised or pot roasted. Allow 175–225 g (6–8 oz) per person.

Silverside A boneless joint needing long, slow cooking, such as boiling or braising. Often salted and cooked as traditional boiled beef and carrots. Allow 175–225 g (6–8 oz) per person.

Brisket Can be sold on or off the bone and is often salted. It is rather a fatty joint from the breast, but has a good flavour. Brisket can be slow-roasted or braised; when salted, it should be boiled. With bone, allow 225–350 g (8–12 oz) per person. Without bone, allow 175–225 g (6–8 oz) per person.

Chuck or blade   A cheaper cut, without bone, fairly lean and suitable for stewing, casseroles and pies. Allow 175–225 g (6–8 oz) per person.

Leg and shin   Cheap, tough cuts, but quite lean and with a good flavour. Long, slow cooking, eg stewing, is needed; these cuts can be used for curries, goulash, stews, meat pies and puddings. Allow 175–225 g (6–8 oz) per person.

ACCOMPANIMENTS

With roast beef serve Yorkshire pudding (see page 103) and horseradish sauce or mustard.

STEAK

PREPARATION OF STEAKS FOR COOKING

Trim the steak to a good shape if necessary and wipe it well. Sprinkle with salt and pepper before cooking. If there is doubt as to its tenderness the steak can be beaten with a rolling pin or steak hammer.

Rump steak   The joint next to the sirloin and one of the commonest cuts used for grilling or frying.

Fillet steak   The undercut of the sirloin, probably one of the best known and most expensive of the cuts used for frying and grilling. Very tender, although it usually has less flavour than rump.

Sirloin steak   Cut into two parts. Porterhouse steak is cut from the thick end of the sirloin, giving a large juicy piece that can weigh 850 g (30 oz); when it is cooked on the bone it is called T-bone steak.

Minute steak is a very thin steak from the upper part of the sirloin, weighing about 150–175 g (5–6 oz), without any fat.

Entrecôte   A steak cut from between the ribs of beef, but a slice cut from the sirloin or rump is often served under this name.

LAMB

HOW TO CHOOSE LAMB

The younger the animal the paler the flesh; in a young lamb it is light pink, while in a mature animal it is light red ■ A slight blue tinge to the bones also suggests the animal is young ■ Imported lamb has a firm, white fat, while English lamb has creamy-coloured fat.

BEEF

shin/leg

silverside

entrecote steak

topside

sirloin

minute steak

rump

fillet steak

rib

forerib

brisket

chuck/blade

Loin A prime cut, usually roasted (or served as chops); can be cooked on or off the bone; if boned, it is usually stuffed and rolled.
Allow 350 g (12 oz) per person on the bone; 125–175 g (4–6 oz) if boned.

Leg Another good roasting cut.
Allow 350 g (12 oz) on the bone per person. The meat is often sold cut from the bone for use in pies, stews, kebabs and so on.

Shoulder A large joint, with more fat but often with more flavour than leg. Usually roasted. Shoulder meat can also be sold off the bone, as for leg.
Allow 350 g (12 oz) on the bone per person.

Best end of neck The cut next to the loin. Very good roasted, or it can be divided into cutlets.
Allow 350 g ($\frac{3}{4}$ lb) per person.

Chops These can be cut from the loin, those nearest the leg being known as chump chops. Suitable for grilling, frying and casseroles.
Allow 1–2 per person.

Cutlets These have a small 'eye' of lean meat and a long bone; suitable for grilling or frying.
Allow 1–2 per person.

Breast A rather fatty cut, therefore usually quite cheap. Usually boned, stuffed and rolled; it can be braised, slow-roasted or stewed.
Allow 225–350 g (8–12 oz) on the bone per person.

Middle and scrag end Cheap cuts with rather a high proportion of bone and fat, but with a good flavour. Suitable for stews and casseroles.
Allow 350 g (12 oz) per person.

ACCOMPANIMENTS

With roast lamb and grilled chops, serve mint sauce or jelly; with roast mutton, redcurrant jelly or onion sauce.
With boiled leg of mutton, caper sauce is traditional.

PORK

HOW TO CHOOSE PORK

The lean part of pork should be pale pink, moist and slightly marbled with fat ■ There should be a good outer layer of firm, white fat, with a thin, elastic skin; if the joint is to be roasted, get the butcher to score the rind ■ The bones should be small and pinkish – denoting a young animal ■ Although pork was considered seasonal at one time, it can now quite safely be bought all the year round.

LAMB

leg

loin

chump chop

best end
of neck

cutlets

scrag end
of neck

shoulder

breast

Leg   A prime joint but rather large, so it is often cut into two. Roasted on the bone, or boned and rolled, sometimes with stuffing.
Allow 225–350 g (8–12 oz) per person with bone; 125–175 g (4–6 oz) without bone.

Fillet end of leg   A lean, expensive cut taken from the top of the hind leg, with a central bone. It is best roasted and can be cooked on the bone or boned and stuffed.
Allow 225–350 g (8–12 oz) on the bone per person.

Loin   An expensive but prime cut, suitable for roasting; it often includes the kidney. It can be cooked on the bone or boned and stuffed.
Allow 225–350 g (8–12 oz) on the bone per person; 125–175 g (4–6 oz) without bone.

Tenderloin (fillet)   A small boneless cut from under the loin, of very tender, lean and delicate meat. Suitable for classic sautés, kebabs and lightly cooked dishes.
Allow 125–175 g (4–6 oz) per person.

Spare rib   Fairly lean and moderately priced. Good for roasting, but can also be cut up for braising and stewing. Also sold as chops or cutlets.
Allow 225–350 g (8–12 oz) on the bone per person.

Spare ribs (American and North-country style) are from the belly and are removed in one piece, leaving the meat between the rib bones. Usually barbecued.

Chops   Usually consist of the cut-up loin and often include the kidney. They can be grilled, fried or casseroled.
Allow 1 per person.

Spare rib chops   These are cut from the spare rib and have little or no bone; they are usually lean. Cutlets are cooked as for chops.
Allow 1 per person.

Blade   Another cut for roasting on the bone.
Allow 225–350 g (8–12 oz) per person.

Belly   A fatty cut, sometimes sold salted; usually boiled and served cold. Can also be roasted.
Allow 100–175 g (4–6 oz) per person.

Hand and spring   The foreleg, suitable for roasting, boiling and stewing.
Allow 350 g (12 oz) per person.

ACCOMPANIMENTS

Apple sauce is the most usual accompaniment, with sage and onion stuffing for roast joints. Baked or fried apples or cranberry or redcurrant jelly make good alternatives.

PORK

fillet or tenderloin

leg

loin

loin chop

belly

sparerib loin chop

American spareribs

spare rib

blade/shoulder .

hand and spring

BACON AND GAMMON

Bacon is made by curing fresh pork and some goes through the additional process of smoking. Bacon joints are equally good hot or cold and any left over makes excellent savouries or supper dishes. Rashers are excellent for meals from breakfast to supper.

Gammon is the hind leg and the most prized part of the bacon side for leanness, flavour and fine texture of the meat. It has little fat. Whole or half gammons are popular for special occasions such as weddings, otherwise they are divided into smaller joints known as middle gammon, corner gammon, and slipper. Often sold as cooked meat.

Back bacon   A prime rasher with a good eye of lean and a distinct layer of fat. Used for frying and grilling and can also be bought in the piece for boiling.

Streaky   Narrow rashers in which lean and fat are mixed. It is good for grilling and frying and provides plenty of fat for frying bread or eggs. Can also be boiled in the piece.

BACON AND GAMMON

middle or through cut bacon

back bacon

streaky

hock or forehock

chops

gammon steak and rashers

collar

gammon joints

Middle or throughcut   Long rashers in which back and streaky are joined. Sold flat or rolled. Good value for family meals and usually priced between back and streaky. With stuffing, it makes a handsome roast or boiling joint.

Bacon chops   Boneless rib back chops cut between 0.5–1 cm ($\frac{1}{4}$–$\frac{1}{2}$ inch) thick. Quick to fry or grill.

Gammon steaks or rashers   Gammon steaks about 1 cm ($\frac{1}{2}$ inch) thick, almost circular in shape, are the leanest and most expensive cuts for frying and grilling.

Collar   Prime collar is one of the best boiling and baking joints and is good for braising. A whole joint weighs about 3.6 kg (8 lb), but it is usually cut into smaller pieces. Collar rashers are substantial and meaty.

Forehock   Small boneless forehock pieces are popular for boiling. Can also be bought with the bone in for roasting, boiling, soups and bacon pieces.

TO BOIL BACON OR GAMMON

Weigh the piece, then calculate the cooking time ■ Tie it if necessary to keep it a good shape. Cover it with water and allow to soak for about 1 hour ■ Place the joint in a large pan and cover with fresh cold water, bring to the boil, then simmer gently until cooked, allowing 20–25 minutes per 450 g (1 lb) plus 20 minutes ■ If you are cooking a large joint, eg a gammon of 4.5 kg (10 lb) or over, allow 15–20 minutes per 450 g (1 lb) plus 15 minutes ■ When the joint is cooked, remove the skin with a knife, if necessary, and serve the meat hot, with parsley sauce ■ Alternatively, allow the joint to cool in the cooking liquid, cut off the outer skin and press browned breadcrumbs into the fat; when the meat is cold, serve with salad or in sandwiches.

TO BAKE GAMMON OR BACON

After weighing the meat and calculating the cooking time, soak as for boiled bacon. Boil for half the cooking time, then drain the joint and wrap in foil ■ Bake at 180°C (350°F) mark 4 until 30 minutes before the cooking time is completed. Raise the oven heat to 220°C (425°F) mark 7 ■ Put 30–45 ml (2–3 level tbsp) brown sugar, 25 g (1 oz) butter and 15 ml (1 tbsp) water in a small saucepan, dissolve and bring to the boil ■ Undo the foil round the bacon, cut off the skin and brush the surface with the sugar glaze; return the joint to the oven and leave until crisp and golden ■ Serve with cranberry sauce or with canned pineapple, peaches or apricots.

ROASTING PORK

To prepare the joint, wash it, trim or stuff as necessary, then weigh to calculate the cooking time – see below. Pork rind should be scored, ie cut with a sharp knife, to produce crackling. For a really crisp effect, rub with oil and salt before cooking.

Scoring pork for crackling

Quick or high-temperature roasting

Heat the oven at 220°C (425°F) mark 7; put the meat in a shallow tin (or on a grid) with the thickest part of any fat uppermost, and roast in the centre of the oven. If there is not much fat, top the meat with 50 g (2 oz) dripping or lard. Time it as follows:

Beef and lamb: 20 minutes per 450 g (1 lb) plus 20 minutes for joints with bone; 25 minutes per 450 g (1 lb) plus 25 minutes for joints without bone.

Pork: 25 minutes per 450 g (1 lb) plus 25 minutes for joints with bone; 30 minutes per 450 g (1 lb) plus 30 minutes for boned joints or veal. Boned and rolled pork is better cooked by the slow method.

Slow or low-temperature roasting

Heat the oven to 190°C (375°F) mark 5.

Beef and lamb: 27 minutes per 450 g (1 lb) plus 27 minutes for joints on the bone; 33 minutes per 450 g (1 lb) plus 33 minutes for joints off the bone.

Pork: All joints are roasted for 30–35 minutes per 450 g (1 lb) plus 35 minutes.

Basting during cooking

BASTING

Two or three times during the cooking spoon the juices and fat from the meat over the joint – this keeps it moist and gives a good flavour. Put fattier joints – especially pork – on a trivet or grid in the meat tin, to keep the melted fat away from the meat.

COVERED ROASTING

Meat can be cooked in a covered roasting tin. This makes the joint more moist and keeps the oven cleaner, though the flavour and colour are not usually quite so good. Roasting in foil also keeps the meat moist and tender, though again the flavour is not usually so good. Extra cooking time is not needed, but the foil should be opened out for the final 30 minutes, to make the joint brown and crisp.

CARVING MEAT

When a joint is well carved it looks attractive and the meat is used in the most economical way. Luckily, carving is an art most people can acquire, given correctly prepared meat and good equipment.

A good butcher will present the joint in the easiest way to carve, if he knows how it is to be served. A joint that includes part of the backbone (eg loin) can be 'chined' – that is, cut through the ribs close to the backbone, leaving a loose piece of bone that is removed before serving.

When preparing meat for cooking never use wooden skewers, which swell and are difficult to remove.

EQUIPMENT

A long-bladed, sharp knife is essential. To restore the sharpness, use a steel or a patent sharpener. To use a steel, draw each side of the blade in turn smoothly down and across with rapid strokes, holding the blade at an angle of 45° to the steel. Take great care, if you are a beginner, not to inflict permanent damage on the knife, and have it expertly reground.

Some stainless steel knives have a hollowed-out, grooved blade; these do not often require sharpening, and are perhaps easier for an inexperienced person, but the skilful carver usually prefers a plain blade.

A sharp two-pronged fork will hold the meat steady; it must have a metal guard to protect the hand in the event of the knife slipping.

A modern meat dish with sharp prongs to hold the joint steady is a great help. Put the meat on the dish with little or no fat and little garnishing. Gravy should be served separately. Place the dish on the table close to the carver and well away from other dishes so that there is room to work.

TECHNIQUE

Each joint must be carved in the way best suited to its structure, to ensure a neat result. The carver must understand the make-up of each joint – where the bone is to be found and how the lean and fat are distributed. The meat is usually best when cut across the grain, though sometimes, when the meat is very tender (as in the undercut of sirloin) the joint is cut with the grain.

It is much easier to carve standing up. Use long, even strokes, keeping the blade at the same angle, to give neat, uniform slices. As you carve, move the knife to and fro, cutting cleanly without bearing down on the meat, which presses out the juices. Serve the meat on to very hot plates or it will cool surprisingly quickly. Beef (except fillet) is carved very thinly, but pork and lamb are cut in slices about 0.5 cm ($\frac{1}{4}$ inch) thick. When cutting a joint with a bone, always take the knife right up to this, so that eventually the bone is left quite clean.

Sirloin Stand the joint on its back with the fillet uppermost; remove the strings. Carve the fillet, loosening each slice from the bone with the knife-tip; turn the joint over and carve in long slices right up to the bone.

Carving flank portion

Cutting towards bone

Rib of beef Stand the joint on edge on the bone. Slice downwards along the full length of the joint, cutting each slice down to the bone and slanting a little away from the cut edge so that the bone is left clean. Support the slices with the fork to prevent them breaking.

Cutting fillet

Cutting wedge-shaped slices

Boneless joints of beef Carve across the grain, usually horizontally. In the case of a long piece of roast fillet, however, you will need to carve downwards.

Best end of neck of lamb Cut the joint right through, downwards, into cutlets. (This joint should be chined.)

Saddle of lamb First carve the meat from the top of the joint in long slices, cutting downwards and parallel with the backbone. Do this at each side of the bone, then carve diagonal slices from either side of the saddle.

Stuffed breast of lamb Cut downwards in fairly thick slices, right through the joint.

Leg of lamb Begin by cutting a wedge-shaped slice from the centre of the meatier side of the joint. Carve slices from each side of the cut, gradually turning the knife to get larger slices and ending parallel to the bone. Turn the joint over and carve in long slices.

Slicing downwards across joint

Carving down to bone

Removing fat

Shoulder of lamb Cut a thick wedge-shaped slice from the centre of the meatiest side of the joint. Carve small slices from each side down to the shank and the shoulder bone. Turn the joint over and carve in long slices.

Cutting slice from centre

Carving to bone

Carving towards shankbone

Loin of pork Sever the chined bone from the chop bones and put to one side. Divide into chops by cutting between the bones and the scored crackling.

Cutting between chined bone and chops

Cutting between bones and crackling

Leg of pork Use the point of the knife to cut through the crackling; it is usually easier to remove it to divide it into portions. Carve as for leg of lamb, but medium thick.

Spare rib of pork Cut between the score marks into moderately thick, even slices.

Boned and rolled pork Remove the string from each part of the joint as it is carved. Cut through the crackling where it was scored half-way along the joint. Lift off the crackling and cut into pieces. Carve the meat into slices.

Lifting off crackling   Carving into slices

HAMBURGERS

Serves 4

450 g (1 lb) lean beef, eg chuck, shoulder or rump
½ onion, skinned and grated (optional)

salt and pepper
melted butter or oil for coating or a little fat for shallow frying

Choose lean meat and have it minced finely by the butcher ■ Mix well with the onion (if used) and a generous amount of salt and pepper. Shape lightly into 6–8 round, flat cakes ■ To cook, brush sparingly with melted butter or oil and grill for 4–6 minutes turning once, or fry in a little fat in a frying pan, turning them once and allowing the same amount of time. Serve rare or well-done according to personal preference.

Shaping into flat cakes

GRILLED STEAK

Serves 4

4 steaks
100 g (4 oz) mushrooms
4 tomatoes

butter or margarine
salt and pepper
oil

Trim the steaks. Trim the mushrooms, halve the tomatoes and put a small knob of butter on each half. Season the mushrooms and tomatoes with salt and pepper ■ Brush the steaks with oil, season with salt and pepper and put them under a preheated grill. Cook under a medium heat, turning them regularly, for the times indicated below ■ Lightly grill mushrooms and tomatoes and arrange with steaks on a serving dish.

Cooking times for steaks (in minutes)

Thickness	Rare	Medium rare	Well-done
2 cm ($\frac{3}{4}$ inch)	5	9–10	12–15
2.5 cm (1 inch)	6–7	10	15
4 cm (1$\frac{1}{2}$ inch)	10	12–14	18–20

STEAK AND MUSHROOM PIE

Serves 4

700 g (1$\frac{1}{2}$ lb) chuck or
    shoulder steak
seasoned flour
1 onion, skinned and
    chopped
100 g (4 oz) mushrooms,
    sliced

300 ml ($\frac{1}{2}$ pint) beef stock
    or water
210-g (7$\frac{1}{2}$-oz) packet
    frozen puff pastry,
    thawed
beaten egg to glaze

Cut the meat in 4-cm (1$\frac{1}{4}$-inch) cubes and toss them in the flour. Put the meat, onion and mushrooms in a pan, add just sufficient liquid to cover, put on lid and cook gently over a low heat until tender – about 1$\frac{1}{2}$ hours. Cool ■ Transfer the meat and vegetables to a 1.4-litre (2$\frac{1}{2}$-pint) pie dish, with enough gravy to half-cover ■ Roll out the puff pastry 2.5 cm (1 inch) larger than the top of the dish and cut off a thin strip for the edge of the pie. Damp the rim of the dish, stick on the pastry strip and put on the top, then seal, trim and decorate the edges. Brush the pastry with a little egg. Bake at 220°C (425°F) mark 7 for 20 minutes. Reduce the temperature to 180°C (350°F) mark 4 and cook for about a further 20 minutes.

Sticking on pastry strip   Putting on top, sealing

BEEF CASSEROLE

Serves 4

Adding liquid to casserole

700 g (1½ lb) stewing steak
30 ml (2 tbsp) vegetable oil
2 onions, skinned and sliced
2–3 carrots, peeled and sliced

60 ml (4 level tbsp) plain flour
900 ml (1½ pints) beef stock
salt and pepper
a bouquet garni

Cut the meat into cubes ■ Heat the oil in a shallow pan and sauté the onions and carrots until golden brown; remove from the pan. Sauté the meat until well browned on all sides. Place the meat and vegetables in a casserole ■ Add the flour to the fat remaining in the pan and cook, stirring, for 1–2 minutes. Add the stock gradually, stirring constantly, then bring to the boil, season and add the bouquet garni. Pour into the casserole and cook in the oven at 170°C (325°F) mark 3 for 2–2½ hours. Remove the bouquet garni before serving.

STEAK AND KIDNEY PUDDING

Serves 4

250 g (9 oz) suetcrust pastry (see page 106)
450 g (1 lb) stewing steak, cut into 2-cm (¾-inch) cubes
2 lamb's kidneys, chopped

15 ml (1 level tbsp) plain flour
salt and pepper
1 small onion, skinned and chopped
45 ml (3 tbsp) beef stock

Half fill a steamer or large saucepan with water and put it on to boil. Grease a 900-ml (1½-pint) pudding basin ■ Roll the pastry out into a round and cut out a quarter of it to keep for the top. Line the pudding basin with the rest – avoid stretching it ■ Toss the meat and kidney in the seasoned flour. Mix with the onion and put into the basin. Pour in the stock ■ Roll out the remaining pastry into a round the size of the top of the basin and damp the edge. Place on the basin and seal carefully. Cover with greased foil and secure with string, then steam for about 4 hours. Serve with a napkin tied round the basin.

Adding meat

Putting on pastry top

Serving

CURRIED BEEF

Serves 4

450 g (1 lb) stewing steak
50 g (2 oz) lard
1 cooking apple, peeled and chopped
2 large onions, skinned and chopped
15 ml (1 level tbsp) curry paste
45 ml (3 level tbsp) plain flour

600 ml (1 pint) beef stock or water
salt and pepper
15 ml (1 level tbsp) chutney
50 g (2 oz) sultanas
2 tomatoes, skinned and quartered
a squeeze of lemon juice
boiled rice

Cut the meat into 2-cm ($\frac{3}{4}$-inch) cubes. Heat the fat in a thick-based saucepan and fry the chopped apple and onions until golden ∎ Add the meat and fry, stirring all the time, until it is browned. Add the curry paste and flour and fry for 2–3 minutes ∎ Gradually add the stock, stir well and boil for 2–3 minutes. Add the seasoning, chutney, sultanas, tomatoes and a squeeze of lemon juice ∎ Cover with a close-fitting lid and simmer gently over a low heat for 2–2$\frac{1}{2}$ hours, or cook in the oven at 170°C (325°F) mark 3, stirring occasionally to prevent the curry sticking to the base of the pan ∎ Before serving, adjust the seasoning as required and place the curry on a hot dish, with a border of boiled rice. Chutney may be served as an accompaniment.

Raw poultry, various meats and vegetables may also be curried in this way. When making a curry of cooked meat, poultry, eggs or vegetables, or of white fish (which requires less cooking), make the curry sauce, cook it for the full time to blend the flavours, then add the cooked food and heat it in the sauce for about 10–15 minutes. Success in curry-making depends on long, slow cooking.

CHILLI CON CARNE

Serves 4–6

700 g (1$\frac{1}{2}$ lb) minced beef
15 ml (1 tbsp) fat or oil
1 large onion, skinned and chopped
1 green pepper, seeded and chopped (optional)
425-g (15-oz) can tomatoes
salt and pepper

15 ml (1 level tbsp) chilli seasoning
15 ml (1 tbsp) vinegar
5 ml (1 level tsp) sugar
30 ml (2 level tbsp) tomato purée
425-g (15-oz) can red kidney beans, drained

Fry the beef in the fat or oil until lightly browned, then add the onion and pepper and fry for 5 minutes until soft ∎ Stir in the tomatoes and add the salt and pepper and the chilli powder mixed with the vinegar, sugar and tomato purée. Cover and simmer for 2–2$\frac{1}{2}$ hours or until tender ∎ Add the kidney beans 10 minutes before the end of the cooking time.

COTTAGE PIE

Serves 4

900 g (2 lb) potatoes
45 ml (3 tbsp) milk
knob of butter
salt and pepper
1 large onion, skinned and
  chopped
little dripping

450 g (1 lb) cold cooked
  beef, minced
stock
30 ml (2 tbsp) chopped
  fresh parsley or 10 ml
  (2 level tsp) mixed
  dried herbs

Boil the potatoes, drain and mash them with the milk, butter and seasoning ■ Fry the onion in a little dripping for about 5 minutes and mix in the minced meat, with a little stock, seasoning and parsley or mixed herbs ■ Put the prepared meat mixture into an ovenproof dish and cover the top with mashed potato. Mark the top with a fork and bake for 25–30 minutes in the oven at 190°C (375°F) mark 5 until the surface is crisp and browned.

GOULASH

Serves 4

700 g (1½ lb) stewing
  steak, cut into 1-cm
  (½-inch) cubes
45 ml (3 level tbsp)
  seasoned flour
2 medium onions, skinned
  and chopped
1 green pepper, seeded
  and chopped
30 ml (2 tbsp) fat or oil
10 ml (2 level tsp) paprika

45 ml (3 level tbsp)
  tomato purée
little grated nutmeg
salt and pepper
50 g (2 oz) plain flour
300 ml (½ pint) beef stock
2 large tomatoes, skinned
  and quartered
bouquet garni
150 ml (¼ pint) beer

Coat the meat with seasoned flour. Fry the onions and pepper lightly in the fat or oil for about 3–4 minutes. Add the meat and fry lightly on all sides until golden brown – about 5 minutes ■ Add the paprika and fry for about a minute longer. Stir in the tomato purée, nutmeg, seasoning and flour and cook for a further 2–3 minutes ■ Add the stock, tomatoes and bouquet garni, put into a casserole and cook in the oven at 170°C (325°F) mark 3 for 1½–2 hours ■ Add the beer, cook for a few minutes longer and remove the bouquet garni. Serve with boiled potatoes and a green salad.

Frying meat lightly

IRISH STEW

Serves 4

450 g (1 lb) middle neck of
  lamb
900 g (2 lb) potatoes,
  peeled and sliced
3 onions, skinned and
  sliced

salt and pepper
beef stock
chopped parsley (optional)

Cut up the meat if necessary and trim off some of the fat. Place alternating layers of meat, potato and onion in a flameproof casserole, finishing with a layer of potato. Season well and add enough stock to half-cover ▪ Cover with a lid and simmer very slowly for 3 hours. If you wish, garnish with chopped parsley before serving.

LAMB KEBABS

Serves 4

thick slice of lamb taken
  from the leg – about
  700 g (1½ lb)
45 ml (3 tbsp) olive oil
15 ml (1 tbsp) lemon juice
salt and pepper
1 garlic clove, skinned and
  crushed

4 small tomatoes, halved
  (optional)
8 button mushrooms
few bay leaves (optional)
2 small onions, quartered
  (optional)
melted butter

Threading skewers

Remove all fat and gristle from the meat and cut it into 2.5-cm (1-inch) cubes. Marinate for 2 hours (or overnight) in the olive oil, lemon juice, seasoning and crushed garlic ▪ Thread 8 skewers alternately with meat cubes, halved tomatoes if using, and whole mushrooms. If you like, a bay leaf or an onion quarter may be placed on each side of the meat pieces to give more flavour. Brush with melted butter and cook under a low grill for 10–15 minutes, turning the kebabs about 3 times, until the meat is tender. Serve on plain boiled rice, with lemon ▪ Lamb's kidneys may also be added; allow ½–1 kidney per person, removing the core. Rolled streaky bacon rashers are another good addition to kebabs. For added flavour, include in the marinade some herbs such as dried marjoram and chopped fresh parsley.

A marinade is a seasoned mixture of oil and vinegar, lemon juice or wine, in which food is left for a given time. This helps to soften the fibres of meat or fish, and adds flavour to the food.

NAVARIN OF LAMB

Serves 4

1 kg (2¼ lb) shoulder of lamb
30 ml (2 tbsp) vegetable oil
5 ml (1 level tsp) sugar
15 ml (1 level tbsp) plain flour
900 ml (1½ pints) beef stock or water
30 ml (2 level tbsp) tomato purée
salt and pepper

bouquet garni
4 onions, skinned and quartered
4 carrots, peeled and sliced
1–2 turnips, peeled and quartered
8 small, even-sized potatoes, peeled
100 g (4 oz) frozen peas (optional)

Trim the meat and cut it into 2.5-cm (1-inch) cubes. Fry it lightly on all sides in the oil. If there is too much fat at this stage, pour off a little to leave 15–30 ml (1–2 tbsp) ■ Stir in the sugar and heat until it browns slightly, then add the flour, stirring until this also cooks and browns. Remove from the heat, stir in the stock gradually, then bring to the boil and add the tomato purée, seasoning and bouquet garni ■ Cover, reduce the heat and simmer for about 1 hour. Remove the bouquet garni, add the onions, carrots and turnips and continue cooking for another 30 minutes. Finally add the potatoes and continue cooking for about 20 minutes, until tender. Add the peas for the last 10 minutes if using ■ Serve the meat on a heated serving dish surrounded by vegetables and garnished with parsley.

MOUSSAKA

Serves 4

2 aubergines, sliced
45–60 ml (3–4 tbsp) olive oil
4–5 medium onions, skinned and sliced
450 g (1 lb) minced raw lamb
4 tomatoes, skinned and sliced

150 ml (¼ pint) beef stock
45 ml (3 level tbsp) tomato purée
2 eggs
45 ml (3 tbsp) milk
45 ml (3 tbsp) cream
salt and pepper

Fry the aubergines in half the oil for about 4–5 minutes, then arrange them in the bottom of an ovenproof dish ■ Fry the onions and meat until lightly browned – about 5 minutes. Place layers of onion and minced meat on top of the aubergines and lastly add the slices of tomato ■ Mix the stock and tomato purée and pour into the dish. Bake in the oven at 180°C (350°F) mark 4 for about 30 minutes ■ Beat together the eggs, milk and cream, season well and pour this mixture over the meat. Put it back into the oven for 15–20 minutes, until the sauce is set and the surface is firm and golden brown.

Layering   Adding slices of tomato

BARBECUED SPARE-RIBS

Serves 4

30 ml (2 tbsp) vegetable
   oil
175 g (6 oz) onions,
   skinned and chopped
1 garlic clove, skinned and
   crushed
30 ml (2 level tbsp)
   tomato purée
60 ml (4 tbsp) vinegar

1.25 ml ($\frac{1}{4}$ level tsp) dried
   thyme
1.25 ml ($\frac{1}{4}$ level tsp) chilli
   seasoning
45 ml (3 level tbsp) honey
1 beef stock cube
1 kg (2$\frac{1}{4}$ lb) spare-ribs
   (American cut)

Heat the oil in a saucepan, add the onion and sauté until clear. Add the flavourings, honey and beef cube, dissolved in 150 ml ($\frac{1}{4}$ pint) hot water. Bubble the mixture gently for 10 minutes ■ Place the spare-ribs in a roasting tin in a single layer. Brush with a little of the sauce; roast in the oven at 190°C (375°F) mark 5 for 30 minutes. Pour off the fat and spoon the remaining sauce over the meat; cook for a further 1–1$\frac{1}{4}$ hours.

PORK AND PRUNE HOT POT

Serves 4

100 g (4 oz) prunes
pared rind and juice of
   1 lemon
450 g (1 lb) boneless pork,
   cut into 2.5-cm (1-inch)
   cubes

25 g (1 oz) seasoned flour
15 g ($\frac{1}{2}$ oz) dripping
salt and pepper

Put the prunes into a saucepan with the lemon rind and sufficient cold water to cover. Bring to the boil and simmer the prunes until they are soft, then drain, reserving the liquid, and stone them ■ Coat the pork cubes in seasoned flour and fry until brown in the dripping. Drain the pork pieces well from the fat, then place in a casserole in layers with the stoned prunes ■ Add the remaining seasoned flour to the fat in the pan and cook, stirring, until brown, then add 300 ml ($\frac{1}{2}$ pint) of the strained liquid, stirring well so that the sauce is smooth ■ Add the lemon juice and seasoning and pour over the meat in the casserole. Cover and cook in the oven at 180°C (350°F) mark 4 for 1 hour. Serve hot from the casserole.

GRILLED PORK CHOPS WITH APPLE RINGS

Serves 4

4 pork chops
olive oil

1 large apple, peeled and
cut in round slices

Trim the chops and brush with oil. Core the apple slices. Place the rings of apple in the base of the grill pan and put the chops on the grid ■ Grill the chops for 8–10 minutes on each side under a medium grill, to make sure that they are well cooked. When they are done, place on a serving dish and keep hot. Put the apple rings on the grid and brown very lightly. Arrange the apple rings between the chops on a serving dish.

GRILLED KIDNEYS

1–2 lamb's or pig's
kidneys per person

oil
salt and pepper

Wash the kidneys. Then remove the skin and cut each kidney in half. Cut out the core with sharp scissors ■ Thread the kidneys on to skewers, cut side uppermost, brush with oil and sprinkle with salt and pepper. Cook under a hot grill for about 6 minutes, uncut side first and then cut side, so that the juices gather in the cut side ■ Serve on fried bread, with grilled or fried bacon, or with fried potatoes.

Coring kidneys

LIVER, BACON AND MUSHROOMS

Serves 4

450 g (1 lb) lamb's or
calf's liver
1–2 onions, skinned and
chopped
4 rashers of lean bacon,
rinded and chopped

25 g (1 oz) fat or oil
100 g (4 oz) mushrooms,
sliced

Wash the liver and cut it into thin strips ■ Fry the onions and bacon in the hot fat or oil for 5 minutes, or until soft, then add the sliced mushrooms and strips of liver and continue frying over a gentle heat, stirring from time to time, for about 5–10 minutes until the meat is just cooked. Drain well before serving.

POULTRY

Thaw a frozen turkey completely before cooking. It is usual to stuff the neck end of a turkey. Allow 450 g (1 lb) for a bird up to 6.3 kg (14 lb), twice this amount for a larger bird.

ROAST TURKEY

1 turkey, frozen or fresh
forcemeat or sausage
   stuffing (see page 102)

dripping or butter
fat bacon rashers

Make the bird as plump and even in shape as possible with the stuffing then truss it with the wings folded under the body and the legs tied together. Before cooking spread the bird with softened dripping or butter; the breast may also be covered with strips of fat bacon ■ If cooking by the quick method (see below) wrap the bird in foil to prevent the flesh drying out and the skin hardening. Foil is not recommended for the slow method of cooking ■ For the slow method roast at 170°C (325°F) mark 3. For the quick method roast at 230°C (450°F) mark 8. Calculate the times by the chart below. Calculate to be ready 30 minutes before serving. If the turkey is cooked, lower the heat and keep the bird hot. If not, continue cooking. Unless the bird is cooked in foil, baste it regularly, turning it round once to ensure even browning. If you use foil, unwrap it for the last 30 minutes, so that the bird may be well basted then left to become crisp and golden ■ Garnish roast turkey with small sausages, forcemeat balls, rolls of bacon and watercress. Serve it with gravy and bread sauce. Cranberry sauce may also be served.

Cooking times

Weight	Hours – slow method	Hours – quick method
2.7–3.6 kg (6–8 lb)	$3-3\frac{1}{2}$	$2\frac{1}{4}-2\frac{1}{2}$
3.6–4.5 kg (8–10 lb)	$3\frac{1}{2}-3\frac{3}{4}$	$2\frac{1}{2}-2\frac{3}{4}$
4.5–5.4 kg (10–12 lb)	$3\frac{3}{4}-4$	$2\frac{3}{4}$
5.4–6.3 kg (12–14 lb)	$4-4\frac{1}{4}$	3
6.3–7.3 kg (14–16 lb)	$4\frac{1}{4}-4\frac{1}{2}$	$3-3\frac{1}{4}$
7.3–8.2 kg (16–18 lb)	$4\frac{1}{4}-4\frac{3}{4}$	$3\frac{1}{4}-3\frac{1}{2}$
9–10 kg (20–22 lb)	$4\frac{3}{4}-5$	$3\frac{1}{2}-3\frac{3}{4}$

TURKEY STROGANOFF

Serves 4

Igniting brandy with taper

450 g (1 lb) turkey fillet
15 ml (1 tbsp) vegetable oil
50 g (2 oz) butter
30 ml (2 tbsp) brandy (optional)
1 garlic clove, skinned and crushed

salt and pepper
1 green pepper, seeded and thinly sliced
225 g (8 oz) button mushrooms, wiped and thinly sliced
60 ml (4 tbsp) soured cream

Thinly slice the turkey ▪ Heat the oil and butter in a large frying pan and brown the turkey strips. Add the brandy if using and ignite it with a taper; when the flames die down, add the crushed garlic and seasoning ▪ Cover the pan and simmer for 4–5 minutes until the turkey is just tender ▪ Increase the heat, add the mushrooms and pepper and cook for 3–4 minutes, turning occasionally ▪ Reduce the heat, stir in the soured cream (if on the thick side, stir before adding to the pan) and adjust the seasoning. Serve hot with rice.

ROAST CHICKEN

Serves 4

1 oven-ready chicken – about 1.5 kg (3¼ lb)
forcemeat or sausage stuffing (see page 102)

6 rashers of streaky bacon, rinded
melted butter or oil
salt and pepper

If the bird is frozen, allow it to thaw completely and remove the giblets from the inside. Wash the inside of the bird, dry with absorbent kitchen paper and stuff it at the neck end. Fold the skin round the neck opening and catch it under the wing tips; tie the legs firmly, brush the chicken with melted butter or oil and sprinkle with salt and pepper. Place 2 rashers of bacon over the breast ▪ Place in a roasting tin. Cook in the oven at 200°C (400°F) mark 6, basting from time to time and allowing 20 minutes per 450 g (1 lb) plus 20 minutes. Put a piece of greaseproof paper over the breast if it shows signs of becoming too brown. Prepare bacon rolls ▪ Using a round bladed knife stretch the rashers, cut in half and roll up. Fifteen minutes before the end of the cooking, remove the bacon from the chicken ▪ Place the bacon rolls in the roasting tin for the remaining 15 minutes. Take the string from the legs before serving ▪ Put the bird on a dish and garnish with bacon rolls. Serve bread sauce and gravy separately.

Removing giblets

Stuffing neck end

Tying legs

CORONATION CHICKEN

Serves 8

2.3-kg (5-lb) chicken, cooked
15 ml (1 tbsp) vegetable oil
1 small onion, skinned and finely chopped
15 ml (1 level tbsp) curry paste
15 ml (1 tbsp) tomato purée

100 ml (4 fl oz) red wine
juice of ½ lemon
4 canned apricot halves, finely chopped
300 ml (½ pint) mayonnaise
100 ml (4 fl oz) whipping cream
salt and pepper
watercress to garnish

Remove all the flesh from the chicken and dice. In a small pan, heat the oil and add the onion and cook for about 3 minutes or until softened. Add the curry paste, tomato purée, wine and lemon juice ■ Simmer, uncovered, for about 10 minutes until well reduced. Strain and cool ■ Sieve the chopped apricot to form a purée. Beat the cooked sauce into the mayonnaise with the apricot purée ■ Lightly whip the cream and fold into the mixture. Season, adding a little extra lemon juice if necessary ■ Toss the chicken pieces into the sauce and serve garnished with watercress.

Dicing chicken flesh

Sieving chopped apricot

Folding cream into mixture

CASSEROLE OF CHICKEN

Serves 4

2 medium onions, skinned and sliced
2 sticks celery, trimmed and chopped
100 g (4 oz) mushrooms, sliced
50 g (2 oz) bacon, rinded and chopped
15 ml (1 tbsp) vegetable oil

25 g (1 oz) butter or margarine
4 chicken joints
45 ml (3 level tbsp) plain flour
450 ml (¾ pint) chicken stock
425-g (15-g) can tomatoes, drained
salt and pepper

Lightly fry the onions, celery, mushrooms and bacon in the oil and butter for about 5 minutes, until golden brown. Remove them from the pan with a slotted spoon and use them to line the bottom of the casserole ■ Fry the chicken joints in the oil and butter for 5 minutes, until golden brown. Put the chicken in the casserole on the bed of vegetables ■ Stir the flour into the fat remaining in the pan and cook for 2–3 minutes; gradually stir in the stock and bring to the boil. Continue to stir until the mixture thickens then add the tomatoes, with salt and pepper to taste ■ Pour this sauce over the chicken joints, cover and cook in the oven at 180°C (350°F) mark 4 for ¾–1 hour, until the chicken is tender.

CREAMY CHICKEN AND TARRAGON PIE

Serves 4

25 g (1 oz) butter or margarine
25 g (1 oz) flour
300 ml (½ pint) milk
salt and pepper
450 g (1 lb) cold cooked chicken, cut into cubes
2.5 ml (½ level tsp) dried tarragon

198-g (7-oz) can sweetcorn, drained
150 ml (¼ pint) soured cream
212-g (7½-oz) packet puff pastry, thawed
beaten egg to glaze

Melt the butter in a pan and stir in the flour. Cook for 2 minutes, stirring. Remove from the heat and stir in the milk. Bring the sauce to the boil and cook for 2 minutes, stirring continuously. Season well and stir in the chicken, tarragon, sweetcorn and soured cream. Pour into a 1.1-litre (2-pint) pie dish ■ Roll out the pastry 5 cm (2 inches) wider than the dish. Cut a 2.5-cm (1-inch) strip from the outer edge and use to line the dampened rim of the pie dish. Dampen the pastry rim with water and cover with the pastry lid, sealing the edges well. Trim and finish. Brush with beaten egg to glaze ■ Bake in the oven at 200°C (400°F) mark 6 for about 30 minutes until the pie crust is golden brown and well risen. Serve hot or cold with a salad or green vegetables.

VEGETABLES AND SALADS

Boiled potatoes

175–225 g (6–8 oz)
    potatoes per person
salt

butter or margarine
chopped parsley

Put the potatoes into salted water and simmer until cooked but unbroken – 15–20 minutes for new potatoes, 20–30 minutes for old ones ■ Drain well, toss with a knob of butter or margarine and serve sprinkled with parsley.

Mashed potatoes

175–225 g (6–8 oz) old
    potatoes per person

salt

Boil the potatoes as above. Drain well and dry over a low heat, then mash with a potato masher or fork, until quite free from lumps.

Mashing potatoes

Creamed potatoes

175–225 g (6–8 oz) old potatoes per person
salt
butter or margarine

45–60 ml (3–4 tbsp) milk
salt and pepper
chopped parsley

Mash the potatoes as above, then add a knob of butter or margarine, milk and a little extra seasoning if necessary. Return them to a gentle heat and beat well with a wooden spoon until fluffy ■ Pile into a dish, mark the top with a fork, and serve sprinkled with chopped parsley.

Potatoes baked in their jackets

1 even-sized potato per person

butter to serve

Scrub each potato well and prick all over with a fork. Bake in the oven at 200°C (400°F) mark 6, for about $\frac{3}{4}$–1 hour, or until they feel soft when squeezed ■ Cut a cross in the top of each potato, put in a knob of butter or a spoonful of soured cream, and serve at once.

Chipped potatoes

175–225 g (6–8 oz) old potatoes per person

oil for deep frying

Cutting potatoes into strips

Wash and peel the potatoes, then cut into 0.5–1-cm ($\frac{1}{4}$–$\frac{1}{2}$-inch) slices. Cut these slices into long strips of 0.5–1 cm ($\frac{1}{4}$–$\frac{1}{2}$ inch) wide. (Several slices can be put on top of one another and cut together for speed.) ■ Place in cold water and leave for at least 30 minutes; drain well and dry with a cloth ■ Put some oil in a deep saucepan or fryer, and heat to 190°C (375°F), or until a chip dropped into the fat rises to the surface straight away, surrounded by bubbles ■ Put enough chips into the basket to about quarter-fill it and lower into the oil ■ Cook for 6–7 minutes. Remove the chips and drain on kitchen paper. Repeat until all the chips are cooked ■ Just before serving, reheat the oil and fry the chips rapidly for about 3 minutes until crisp and golden outside and tender inside. Drain well on kitchen paper and serve in an uncovered dish.

Roast potatoes

175–225 g (6–8 oz) old potatoes per person

100 g (4 oz) lard or dripping

Wash, peel and cut into even-sized pieces. Cook in salted water for 5–10 minutes (depending on size). Drain well, then carefully transfer to a roasting tin containing hot lard or dripping. Baste well and bake in the oven at 220°C (425°F) mark 7 for 20 minutes, then turn them and continue cooking for a further

20 minutes or until tender inside and crisp and brown outside. Drain well on kitchen paper, put into a serving dish, sprinkle with salt and serve at once.

If preferred, the potatoes need not be parboiled first (in this case they will take 50–60 minutes to cook); they may also be cooked in the roasting tin around the meat, when little or no extra fat will be needed.

Sauté potatoes

175–225 g (6–8 oz) potatoes, per person, boiled

butter or lard
chopped parsley or chives

Cut the potatoes into rounds 0.5 cm ($\frac{1}{4}$ inch) thick, and fry in a little hot butter or lard, turning once, until crisp and golden on both sides ■ Drain well and serve at once, sprinkled with parsley or chives.

Frying potatoes in hot butter

Spring greens

Separate the leaves and cut off the base of any thick stems. Wash well, then shred roughly. Cook as for cabbage. Chop before serving if you wish.
Allow 225 g (8 oz) per person.

Brussels sprouts

Remove the outer leaves, cut a cross in the bottom of the stems, wash, then cook rapidly in boiling salted water for about 10–15 minutes, or until just cooked. Drain well, then toss with a little butter or margarine and a sprinkling of pepper.
Allow 100–175 g (4–6 oz) per person.

Cutting cross in stems

Vegetable marrow

Peeling marrow

Peel the marrow, remove the seeds and cut the flesh into large cubes. Cook in a little boiling salted water for 10–20 minutes, until soft; drain really well. Toss with butter and a sprinkling of pepper and chopped parsley or coat with a well-seasoned white or cheese sauce (see page 94).

Alternatively, cut the marrow into large dice; melt about 25 g (1 oz) butter in a saucepan, add the marrow, season and cover tightly. Cook over a low heat, shaking the pan occasionally, for 10–20 minutes. Garnish with chopped parsley.

Marrow can also be roasted in the dripping round the meat or stuffed and baked either whole or in rings (see page 71).

Allow 175 g (6 oz) per portion.

Savoy and Dutch cabbage

Remove the coarse outer leaves, cut the cabbage in half and cut out the hard centre stalk. Wash thoroughly, shred the leaves finely, and cook rapidly in about 2.5 cm (1 inch) boiling salted water for 5–10 minutes, or until just done. Drain well and toss with a knob of butter or margarine, a sprinkling of pepper and a pinch of grated nutmeg (optional). Serve at once.

Allow 175–225 g (6–8 oz) per person.

For salads, wash the leaves in cold salted water. Drain well and shred finely.

Cutting out centre stalk   Shredding leaves

Red cabbage   Cook as above but add 15 ml (1 tbsp) vinegar to the water to improve the flavour; allow 15–20 minutes cooking.

Spinach

Remove the stalks and any damaged leaves and wash very thoroughly in several waters, to remove grit or mud. Pack it into a saucepan with only the water that clings to it, heat gently turning the spinach occasionally, then bring to the boil and cook gently for 5–10 minutes until tender. Drain thoroughly, add a small knob of butter or margarine and some salt and pepper before serving.

Allow 225 g (8 oz) per person.

Cauliflower

Remove any coarse outer leaves, but leave the small ones intact. Trim the base of the stem and cut a cross in it, then wash the cauliflower well. Cook, stem side down, in fast-boiling salted water to come half-way up for 10–15 minutes, depending on the size. Drain well and, if liked, serve coated with a white or cheese sauce (see page 98).

The cauliflower can be divided into individual florets and cooked in fast-boiling water for 8–10 minutes. Drain well and serve tossed with butter or margarine and a sprinkling of pepper or coated with sauce.

A medium cauliflower serves 4 people.

Cutting cross in base of stem

Courgettes

These are a variety of small vegetable marrow. They are normally cooked unpeeled, either left whole or cut into rounds. They may be boiled in a minimum of water (allow 10–15 minutes), steamed or fried and are served with melted butter and chopped parsley or tarragon. Alternatively cook, dress with French dressing while still warm, then leave to go cold and serve as a salad.

Allow 100 g (4 oz) per portion.

French and runner beans

French Top, tail and wash the beans. Cook whole, or cut in half if large, in boiling salted water until tender but still crisp – 8–12 minutes for young beans, 15–20 minutes for larger ones.

Runner Top, tail and string the beans. Cut diagonally into 1 cm ($\frac{1}{2}$ inch) slices or slice thinly lengthways. Cook in boiling salted water for about 10 minutes until tender.

French and runner beans should be served tossed in butter or margarine with a sprinkling of pepper.

Allow 100–225 g (4–8 oz) per person.

Stringing the beans

Peas

Shell the peas, wash and place in boiling salted water with 5 ml (1 level tsp) sugar and a sprig of fresh mint. Cook till tender – 8–10 minutes; drain, take out the mint and add a small knob of butter or margarine. Allow about 225 g (8 oz) peas in the pod per person.

Broad beans

Shell the beans, cook them in boiling salted water for 15–20 minutes until tender and drain. Serve with parsley sauce or tossed with a knob of butter or margarine and a little chopped parsley. Allow 225–350 g (8–12 oz) beans in the shell per person.

Mushrooms

Wiping the mushrooms

The majority of mushrooms bought today are cultivated and need only wiping before being used. Cut off and discard the earthy end of each stalk. Field mushrooms need skinning and should be washed thoroughly to remove any mud or grit. Allow 25–75 g (1–3 oz) per person, depending on whether the mushrooms are used as a garnish or a vegetable.
For salads, wipe or skin as necessary, trim the base of the stalks and halve or slice.

Slicing mushrooms

Grilled   Wipe the mushrooms and trim the stalks level with the caps. Melt 50 g (2 oz) butter or margarine per 450 g (1 lb) mushrooms. Dip the caps in butter and grill cap uppermost for 2 minutes. Turn them, sprinkle with salt and pepper and grill for a further 2–3 minutes.

Sauté   Prepare the mushrooms, leaving them whole or cutting in slices as preferred. Cook gently until soft in about 25 g (1 oz) butter or margarine with some salt and pepper; shake them from time to time. A squeeze of lemon juice can be added just before serving.

Baked   Place the prepared whole mushrooms stalks uppermost, in a greased ovenproof dish, dot with butter or margarine, add a little salt and pepper, then cover with foil or greaseproof paper and bake in the oven at 190°C (375°F) mark 5 for 15–30 minutes, or until cooked.

Turnips

Peel rather thickly, cut either in pieces or dice and put immediately under water to prevent discoloration. Cook in salted water until tender; the time will vary considerably, from 20–45 minutes, according to their age and whether the pieces are large or small. Drain and add pepper and a little butter or margarine; they may also be mashed. Young turnips may be left whole. Allow 100–175 g (4–6 oz) per person.

Parsnips

Peel these thinly and cut into quarters, or into even-sized pieces if large and remove any hard centre core. They are very good cooked in the dripping round roast meat – allow about 1 hour. Otherwise, boil them in salted water until tender, allowing about 30 minutes. Drain and toss with a knob of butter or margarine and some grated nutmeg or chopped parsley. Alternatively, mash the parsnips well with butter and pepper.
Allow 175–225 g (6–8 oz) per person.

Carrots

Dice, strips, rounds

New Trim off the leaves, then scrape lightly with a sharp knife. Small new carrots are usually cooked whole. Simmer in salted water for about 15 minutes or until cooked and serve tossed with a little butter or margarine, pepper and chopped parsley.

Old Peel thinly and cut into 0.5–1 cm ($\frac{1}{4}$–$\frac{1}{2}$ inch) lengthways strips; these strips can then be cut across into small dice. Alternatively, cut them into thin rounds. Simmer in salted water until tender – 10–15 minutes for strips and cubes, 6–8 minutes for thin slices.
For salads, pare and cut into thin rings if new, or grate (using the large holes of the grater) if old.
Allow 100–175 g (4–6 oz) per person.

Leeks

Remove the coarse outer leaves and cut off the roots and green tops. Split the leaf end down so that the leeks can be thoroughly washed and any soil or grit removed. Cook in boiling salted water until just tender – about 10–15 minutes – then drain very thoroughly. Serve coated with a white or cheese sauce.
Allow 1–3 leeks or 225–350 g (8–12 oz) per person, depending on the amount of waste.

Trimming roots and splitting leaves

Swedes

These are prepared and cooked like turnips. They are sometimes diced and cooked with diced turnips or carrots.
Allow 175–225 g (6–8 oz) per person.

Beetroots

Cut off the leaves, leaving 2.5 cm (1 inch) of stem and taking care not to damage the skins. Wash the beetroots and boil them in salted water until tender; small, early beetroots will take about 30 minutes, larger, older ones about 1½ hours. Peel off the skin, cut off the stems and roots and cut the beetroot into cubes or slices; serve hot, coated with a white sauce, or leave to cool, then serve sliced in a little vinegar. Beetroot can be bought ready cooked. Peel thinly, then dice or grate. Put in a small dish, sprinkle with salt and pepper and cover with vinegar. Allow 100 g (4 oz) per person.

Celery

Washing celery with brush

Wash celery thoroughly, using a brush to remove all soil from the grooves of the outer stalks. Cut the stalks in even lengths and cook in boiling salted water until tender, 10–20 minutes depending on the coarseness of the celery. Drain carefully and serve with a white, parsley, or cheese sauce (see page 98). Allow 1 head of celery per person if small, 2–3 sticks if large.

For salad, separate the sticks and scrub well in cold water to remove any dirt. Slice, chop or make into 'curls', as follows. Cut into strips about 0.5 cm (¼ inch) wide and 5 cm (2 inch) long. Make cuts along the length of each strip, close together and to within 1 cm (½ inch) of one end. Leave the pieces in cold water for 1–2 hours, until the strips curl.

Tomatoes

Grilled Choose even-sized tomatoes; halve and place on the grid in the grill pan, cut side uppermost. Put a small piece of butter or margarine and a sprinkling of salt and pepper on each and cook under medium heat for 5–10 minutes, depending on their size until soft.

Baked Prepare as for grilled tomatoes or if of even size leave whole and cut a cross just through the skin, on the end away from the stem. Place in a greased ovenproof dish. Brush with melted butter or margarine and sprinkle with salt and pepper, cover with foil or greaseproof paper and bake in the oven at 180°C (350°F) mark 4 for 10–15 minutes. Allow 1–2 tomatoes per person, or 450 g (1 lb) for 4.

Peeling off tomato skin

TO SKIN TOMATOES
Dip them in a pan of boiling water for a minute, then place in a basin of cold water – the skin should then peel off easily.

For salads, slice thinly or cut into 6–8 segments.

Onions

Cut off the roots and remove the thin, papery brown skin. (Use a fork to prevent the smell clinging to hands.) Cook in boiling salted water for 30–40 minutes according to size, drain well and serve with a white or cheese sauce (see page 98).
Allow 100–175 g (4–6 oz) per person.
For salads use spring onions. Trim off the root end, remove the papery outer skins and trim the green leaves down to about 5 cm (2 inch).

Removing outer skin of onion

Lettuce

Separate the leaves and wash them under a running cold tap or in a bowl of cold water. Drain the lettuce by shaking it in a clean tea-towel or colander.

Cucumber

Wipe the skin and either leave it on or peel very thinly. Cut into very thin slices. To give a deckled effect, cut thin strips from the skin with a sharp knife before slicing the cucumber.

Cress

Trim off the roots and lower part of the stems with scissors and place the leaves in a colander or sieve. Wash (under a fast-running cold tap, if possible), turning the cress over to remove any seeds. Drain.

Watercress

Trim the coarse ends from the stalks and place the watercress in a bowl of cold water, adding 10 ml (2 level tsp) salt. Drain well.

Trimming ends from stalks

Herbs (eg parsley or mint)

Remove any large stems, wash the leaves in a colander or sieve, shake and allow to drain well, then chop with a cook's knife.

Radishes

Trim off the root end and leaves, place the radishes in cold water and rub well to remove any dirt. Leave whole, if small; if large, slice thinly into rings or make into flowers.

Trimming and slicing

FRENCH DRESSING

salt and pepper
2.5 ml (½ level tsp) mustard
a pinch of sugar

15 ml (1 tbsp) vinegar
45 ml (3 tbsp) olive or vegetable oil

Put the salt, pepper, mustard and sugar together in a basin, add the vinegar and mix well, then blend in the olive oil, using a fork.

This is the dressing most commonly used for green salads (see page 69) and for simple mixed salads. It may be varied in several ways – for example:

With parsley or other herbs or flavourings   Make French dressing in the usual way and add some freshly chopped parsley, mint or other fresh herbs. Chopped gherkins, pickles or garlic can also be included in the dressing, to add interest and flavour.

With chopped olives   Chop a few stuffed olives and add to French dressing made as above.

MAYONNAISE

Makes about 150 ml (¼ pint)

1 egg yolk
2.5 ml (½ level tsp) dry mustard
salt and pepper
2.5 ml (½ level tsp) sugar

about 150 ml (¼ pint) olive or vegetable oil
15 ml (1 tbsp) white wine vinegar or lemon juice

Put the egg yolk into a basin with the seasonings and sugar. Mix thoroughly, then add the oil drop by drop, stirring briskly with a wooden spoon the whole time or using a whisk, until the sauce is thick and

Adding oil drop by drop

smooth ■ If it becomes too thick add a little of the vinegar. When all the oil has been added, add the vinegar or lemon juice gradually and mix thoroughly.

To keep the basin firmly in position while you whisk in the oil, twist a damp cloth tightly round the base. Should the sauce curdle while you are making it, put another egg yolk into a basin and add the curdled sauce very gradually, in the same way as the oil is added to the original egg yolks.

GREEN SALAD

Use two or more green salad ingredients, such as lettuce, cress, watercress, endive, chicory or cabbage. Wash and drain them and just before serving toss lightly in a bowl with French dressing (see page 68), adding a little finely chopped onion if you wish ■ Sprinkle with chopped fresh parsley, chives, mint, tarragon or other herbs as available.

COLESLAW

Serves 4

$\frac{1}{4}$ of a hard white cabbage
$\frac{1}{2}$ a green pepper
2–3 sticks of celery
1 red-skinned eating apple

salad cream or
 mayonnaise (see
 page 68)

Shred the cabbage finely, cut the pepper into thin strips, chop the celery and dice the apple or cut in segments ■ Mix all these ingredients together and bind with salad cream. Serve garnished with a few strips of green pepper and segments of apple.
Note: 25–50 g (1–2 oz) finely chopped walnuts or 50 g (2 oz) sultanas can be included.

ORANGE SALAD

Serves 4

2 oranges
a little chopped tarragon
 and chervil, or chopped
 mint
10 ml (2 tsp) wine vinegar

15 ml (1 tbsp) olive or
 vegetable oil
5 ml (1 tsp) lemon juice
watercress to garnish

Peel the oranges, removing all the skin and white pith, and cut into segments or cut them across thinly into rounds using a serrated knife ■ Put them into a shallow dish and sprinkle with a mixture of chopped tarragon and chervil, or with mint ■ Blend together the oil, vinegar and lemon juice, pour over the fruit and allow to stand for a short time ■ To serve, lay the oranges on a bed of watercress and spoon the dressing over.

TOMATO SALAD

Serves 4

4 tomatoes
a little chopped onion
salt and pepper
30 ml (2 tbsp) olive or
    vegetable oil

15 ml (1 tbsp) vinegar
chopped fresh parsley
    (optional)

Skin the tomatoes and slice them fairly thinly ■
Arrange in a dish, sprinkle with chopped onion and
seasoning and add the mixed oil and vinegar. Sprinkle
with parsley if you wish.

POTATO SALAD

Serves 4

225 g (8 oz) cooked
    potatoes
2–3 spring onions
salad cream or
    mayonnaise (see
    page 68)

finely chopped parsley or
    chives
watercress (optional)

Dice the potatoes and slice the spring onions ■
Mix both with salad cream, pile into a dish, sprinkle
with parsley or chives and garnish, if liked, with
watercress.

WINTER SALAD

Serves 4

3–4 sticks celery
1 cooked beetroot
1 eating apple
½ a small onion

salad cream or
    mayonnaise (see
    page 68)

Wash and chop the celery; peel and dice the beetroot;
quarter, core and dice the apple; grate or finely chop
the onion ■ Mix these ingredients together and
add just enough salad cream to bind.

SUPPER DISHES

MUSHROOMS ON TOAST

Serves 2

225 g (8 oz) mushrooms
15 ml (1 tbsp) lemon juice
   or 5 ml (1 tsp)
   Worcestershire sauce
25 g (1 oz) butter

salt and pepper
a little cream or top of the
   milk
fingers of hot toast
chopped fresh parsley

Chop the mushrooms, put them in a small pan, just cover with water and add the lemon juice or Worcestershire sauce and butter; season to taste. Cook gently until the water has evaporated, then keep hot ■ Just before serving, stir in the cream or top of the milk, place the mixture on the fingers of toast and garnish with a little chopped parsley.

CHICKEN LIVERS ON TOAST

Serves 2

75–100 g (3–4 oz)
   chicken livers
seasoned flour
butter for frying

50 g (2 oz) sliced
   mushrooms (optional)
½ glass sherry or Madeira
2 slices bread, toasted

Wash and dry the livers, cut them in small pieces and coat with the seasoned flour ■ Melt some butter in a frying pan and fry the bread for 2–3 minutes, until golden on both sides. Put in the prepared livers and mushrooms if used and stir them over the heat until browned ■ Add the sherry or Madeira, mix and cook for 10–15 minutes. Serve on toast.

STUFFED MARROW

Serves 4

Cutting into slices

1 vegetable marrow,
   about 1 kg (2¼ lb)
350 g (12 oz) cold cooked
   meat, minced
60 ml (4 level tbsp) fresh
   breadcrumbs
1 onion, skinned and finely
   chopped

5–10 ml (1–2 level tsp)
   mixed dried herbs or
   15 ml (1 tbsp) chopped
   fresh parsley
salt and pepper
1 egg, beaten
tomato sauce (see
   page 101)

Wash the marrow, peel and cut into slices 4–5 cm (1½–2 inches) thick. Remove the seeds and stand the pieces in a greased ovenproof dish ■ Mix the minced meat, crumbs, herbs, onion and seasoning with a fork and add enough egg to bind the mixture together ■ Put this stuffing into the marrow rings, cover with foil and bake in the oven at 180°C (350°F) mark 4 for about 15–20 minutes, until tender.

STUFFED AUBERGINES

Serves 4

2 medium aubergines
50 g (2 oz) cooked ham, chopped
15 ml (1 tbsp) chopped fresh parsley
1 tomato, skinned and chopped
50 g (2 oz) fresh breadcrumbs
½ onion, skinned and grated
salt and pepper
100 g (4 oz) Cheddar cheese, grated
little stock or beaten egg

Scooping out flesh from halves

Wash the aubergines and remove the stalks. Cut in half lengthways and scoop out the flesh from the centre of each, leaving a 0.5-cm (¼-inch) thick 'shell' ■ Make the stuffing by combining the ham, parsley, tomato, crumbs, onion, seasoning and half the grated cheese with the roughly chopped aubergine flesh. Moisten with a little stock or beaten egg and fill the aubergine shells ■ Sprinkle with the remaining grated cheese, cover with a lid or foil and bake in the oven at 200°C (400°F) mark 6 for 30 minutes, or until cooked. Uncover and cook for a further 5–10 minutes, until crisp and brown on top. Serve hot with a cheese or tomato sauce (see pages 98 and 101).

SAUSAGE ROLLS

Makes about 16

212-g (7½-oz) packet frozen puff pastry, thawed
225 g (8 oz) sausagemeat
flour
egg to glaze

Roll out the pastry to about 0.2 cm ($\frac{1}{16}$ inch) thick; make it into an oblong 15 cm (6 inches) wide and cut this into two ■ Divide the sausagemeat into 2 portions and dust each lightly with flour. Roll into 2 'sausages' the length of the strips of pastry ■ Lay a roll of sausage down the centre of each strip, brush each side of the pastry with egg, then fold one side of the pastry over the meat ■ Press the two edges firmly together and seal by making horizontal cuts with a knife. Glaze with beaten egg. Cut into pieces 4–5 cm (1½–2 inches) long, place on a baking sheet and cook in the oven at 200°C (400°F) mark 6 for 30 minutes.

Cutting the pastry in two

Brushing pastry with egg

Sealing the edges

EGG AND CHEESE DISHES

QUICK PIZZA

Serves 2–3

100 g (4 oz) self raising flour
2.5 ml (½ level tsp) salt
75 ml (5 tbsp) vegetable oil
45–60 ml (3–4 tbsp) water
1 small onion, skinned and chopped
5–10 ml (1–2 level tsp) dried mixed herbs
25 g (1 oz) butter or margarine

396-g (14-oz) can tomatoes, drained and chopped or 450 g (1 lb) fresh tomatoes, skinned and chopped
100 g (4 oz) Cheddar cheese, cut in small cubes
few olives and anchovy fillets

Spreading cheese

Mix the flour and salt and stir in 15 ml (1 tbsp) oil and enough water to mix to a fairly soft dough. Roll out to an 18-cm (7-inch) round and fry on one side in the remaining oil in a large frying pan ▪ Meanwhile make the topping by frying the onion, tomatoes and herbs in the butter or margarine. Turn the dough over and spread with the tomato mixture, the cheese and a few sliced olives and/or anchovy fillets ▪ Fry until the underside is golden and place under a hot grill until the cheese is golden and bubbling. Serve hot, cut in wedges.

HAM AND LEEKS AU GRATIN

Serves 4

4 large or 8 small leeks
salt
25 g (1 oz) butter or margarine
45 ml (3 level tbsp) plain flour

300 ml (½ pint) milk
75 g (3 oz) Cheddar cheese, grated
4–8 slices cooked ham

Wrapping ham round leek

Prepare the leeks by trimming the leaves and cutting off the roots; split then wash thoroughly under running water ▪ Cook in boiling salted water for 10–15 minutes until just tender; drain well ▪ Melt the butter, stir in the flour and cook for 2–3 minutes, then gradually add the milk. Bring to the boil, stirring constantly, and simmer for 5 minutes; remove from the heat and add two-thirds of the grated cheese ▪ Wrap a slice of ham round each leek and place in an ovenproof dish, pour the cheese sauce over and sprinkle the remaining grated cheese on top. Brown lightly under a hot grill.

COURGETTE AND CHEESE FLAN

Serves 4–6

Lining flan dish

Trimming surplus pastry

Beating cream and egg yolks

175 g (6 oz) plain flour
15 ml (1 level tbsp) grated Parmesan cheese
2.5 ml ($\frac{1}{2}$ level tsp) dry mustard
1.25 ml ($\frac{1}{4}$ level tsp) paprika
175 g (6 oz) butter or margarine
about 30 ml (6 tsp) cold water
450 g (1 lb) small courgettes, trimmed and sliced
1 garlic clove, skinned and crushed
grated rind of $\frac{1}{2}$ a lemon
10 ml (2 tsp) lemon juice
salt and pepper
45 ml (3 level tbsp) plain flour
150 ml ($\frac{1}{4}$ pint) milk
142 ml (5 fl oz) soured cream
1 egg, separated
175 g (6 oz) mature Cheddar cheese, grated
snipped chives to garnish

Sift the flour, Parmesan, mustard and paprika together. Rub in half the fat with your fingertips, add about 30 ml (6 tsp) cold water and knit the dough together with your fingertips ■ Roll it out and use to line a 23-cm (9-inch) fluted flameproof flan dish. Bake blind (see page 106) in the oven at 200°C (400°F) mark 6 for about 25 minutes ■ Blanch the courgettes for 1 minute in boiling water, then drain ■ Melt 50 g (2 oz) butter or margarine in a frying pan and add the courgettes, garlic, lemon rind and lemon juice. Season and fry slowly until the courgettes are soft. Lift out the courgettes with a slotted spoon and put them aside on a plate ■ Add the remaining fat to the pan, stir in the flour and cook for 2–3 minutes. Remove from the heat and stir in the milk gradually. Bring to the boil, reduce the heat and cook for a few minutes. Beat in the soured cream and egg yolk. Cool slightly ■ Whisk the egg white stiffly, fold it into the sauce with the cheese and check the seasoning. Spread the sauce over the base of the flan case and top with the courgettes. Bake in the oven at 200°C (400°F) mark 6 for 10–15 minutes. Garnish with chives before serving.

CHEESE ON TOAST

Serves 2

2 thick slices of bread
butter
100 g (4 oz) Cheddar, Lancashire, or Cheshire cheese, grated
salt and pepper
1.25 ml ($\frac{1}{4}$ level tsp) dry mustard or a few drops of Worcestershire sauce
a little milk to mix
2 tomatoes, halved

Toast and butter the bread and keep warm ■ Mix the cheese and seasonings with enough milk to make a spreadable mixture. Pile on to the toast, taking it right to the edges ■ Cook under a hot grill until golden and bubbly; grill the tomatoes at the same time. Serve the toast garnished with tomatoes.

QUICHE LORRAINE

Serves 4

shortcrust pastry made
  with 150 g (5 oz) flour
  etc (see page 104)
75–100 g (3–4 oz) lean
  bacon, rinded and
  chopped
75–100 g (3–4 oz)
  Gruyère or Cheddar
  cheese, thinly sliced

2 eggs, beaten
150 ml ($\frac{1}{4}$ pint) single
  cream or milk
salt and pepper

Roll out the pastry and use it to line an 18-cm (7-inch) plain flan ring or sandwich cake tin, making a double edge ■ Cover the bacon with boiling water and leave for 2–3 minutes, then drain well. Put into the pastry case with the cheese; mix the eggs and cream, season well and pour into the case ■ Bake in the oven at 200°C (400°F) mark 6 for about 30 minutes, until well risen and golden.

BAKED EGGS

Serves 4

butter or margarine
4 eggs

salt and pepper

Place small pieces of butter or margarine in individual dishes and put in the oven to melt. Break the eggs one at a time and put in the dishes. Season lightly and bake in the oven at 180°C (350°F) mark 4 for 5–8 minutes or until the eggs are just set.

EGGS FLORENTINE

Serves 4

900 g (2 lb) spinach
salt and pepper
40 g (1$\frac{1}{2}$ oz) butter or
  margarine
45 ml (3 level tbsp) plain
  flour

300 ml ($\frac{1}{2}$ pint) milk
75 g (3 oz) Cheddar
  cheese, grated
4 eggs

Wash the spinach well in several changes of water, put into a saucepan with a little salt and just the water that clings to the leaves. Cover and cook for 5–10 minutes, until tender. Drain well, chop roughly and reheat with a knob of butter. Melt the remaining butter, stir in the flour and cook for 2–3 minutes. Remove the pan from the heat and gradually stir in the milk; bring to the boil and continue to stir until the sauce thickens ■ Add 50 g (2 oz) cheese and season. Poach the eggs (see page 13) ■ Place the spinach in an ovenproof dish, arrange the eggs on top and pour the cheese sauce over. Sprinkle with the remaining cheese and brown under the grill.

OMELETTE

Serves 1

2 eggs
10–20 ml (2–4 tsp) water

salt and pepper
15 g (1½ oz) butter

Lightly whisk together the eggs, water and some seasoning ■ Heat the butter in a frying pan, tilting it so that the inside surface is evenly greased. Pour in the egg mixture and gently stir the mixture towards the centre with a fork, keeping the back of the prongs flat against the base of the pan, so that the uncooked egg can flow to the sides of the pan and cook ■ Once the egg has set, stop stirring and cook the omelette for another minute, until the underside is golden brown ■ Using a palette knife, fold one-third towards the centre, then fold the opposite third to the centre. Turn the omelette on to a warm plate, with the folded sides underneath.

Stirring mixture with fork   Folding omelette

Omelette fillings

Fines herbes   Add 5 ml (1 level tsp) mixed dried herbs or 10 ml (2 tsp) finely chopped fresh herbs to the beaten egg mixture before cooking. Parsley, chives, chervil and tarragon are all suitable.

Cheese   Grate 40 g (1½ oz) cheese and mix 45 ml (3 tbsp) of it with the eggs before cooking. Sprinkle the rest over the omelette after it is folded.

Tomato   Skin and chop 1–2 tomatoes and fry in a little butter in a saucepan for 5 minutes, until soft and pulpy. Put in the centre of the omelette before folding.

Mushroom   Wash and slice 50 g (2 oz) mushrooms and cook in butter in a saucepan until soft. Put in the centre of the omelette before folding.

SCOTCH EGGS

Serves 4

4 eggs, hard-boiled and
   shelled
10 ml (2 level tsp)
   seasoned flour
Worcestershire sauce

225 g (8 oz) sausagemeat
1 egg, beaten
dry breadcrumbs
fat for deep frying
fresh parsley

Dust the eggs with seasoned flour. Add a few drops of Worcestershire sauce to the sausagemeat and divide it into four equal portions. Form each portion into a flat cake and work it round an egg, making it as even as possible, to keep the egg a good shape and making sure there are no cracks in the sausagemeat. Brush with beaten egg and toss in the crumbs ■ Heat the fat until it will brown a cube of bread in 40–50 seconds. Fry the eggs for 7–8 minutes. When they are golden brown on the outside, remove them from the fat and drain ■ Cut the eggs in half lengthways, garnish each half with a small piece of parsley and serve either hot with tomato sauce (see page 101) or cold with a green salad.

Working sausagemeat round egg

Cutting eggs in half lengthways

EGGS À LA MORNAY

Serves 4

40 g (1½ oz) butter or
    margarine
45 ml (3 level tbsp) flour
300 ml (½ pint) milk
salt and pepper
50 g (2 oz) Cheddar
    cheese, grated

4 eggs, hard-boiled and
    sliced
chopped fresh parsley to
    garnish

Melt 25 g (1 oz) butter in a saucepan, stir in flour and cook gently for 1 minute, stirring. Remove the pan from the heat and gradually stir in the milk. Bring to the boil and continue to cook, stirring until the sauce thickens. Season well and stir in 25 g (1 oz) cheese ■ Lay the eggs in an ovenproof dish, reserving a few slices to garnish. Pour over the sauce, sprinkle the remaining cheese on top and dot with the remaining butter ■ Place under a hot grill and grill for 2–3 minutes until brown. Serve garnished with the reserved slices of egg and chopped parsley.

SAVOURY PANCAKES

Serves 4

Coating pan with batter

Turning with palette knife

Filling and rolling pancakes

125 g (4 oz) plain flour
pinch of salt
1 egg
300 ml (½ pint) milk or
milk and water
fat for frying

For the filling
1 onion, skinned and
quartered
2 carrots, peeled and
quartered

2 sticks of celery,
scrubbed
450 g (1 lb) cold cooked
beef
298-g (10½-oz) can oxtail
soup or 150 ml (¼ pint)
beef stock
salt and pepper
30 ml (2 level tbsp) curry
powder
50 g (2 oz) raisins or
sultanas

Make a batter by mixing the flour and salt and beating in the egg and about 30 ml (2 tbsp) milk or milk and water until smooth. Gradually beat in the remaining liquid to give a creamy batter ■ Then make the filling. Mince together the vegetables and meat (or if you prefer dice the vegetables and mince the meat). Put them in a pan and stir in enough of the soup or stock to give a really moist mixture. Add the seasoning, curry powder and raisins or sultanas, cover with a lid and simmer gently for 20–30 minutes, until the vegetables are soft and the flavours well blended. Stir from time to time as the mixture tends to stick slightly; add more soup or stock if it becomes too thick ■ Melt just enough fat in a thick based frying pan and when it is hot pour in just enough batter to coat the base of the pan – about 30–45 ml (2–3 tbsp). Cook over a medium heat until brown underneath, then turn, using a palette knife, and brown the second side. Keep the pancakes hot in a warm oven and when they are all made, spread with the filling, roll up and serve at once.

EGG MAYONNAISE

Serves 4

4 eggs, hard-boiled and
shelled
few lettuce leaves
150 ml (¼ pint)
mayonnaise (see
page 68)

chopped fresh parsley or
paprika

Cut the eggs lengthways into halves. Wash and drain the lettuce and put on a shallow dish ■ Serve the eggs on the lettuce, cut side down; coat with mayonnaise and garnish with parsley or paprika.

RICE
AND PASTA

RICE

There are three main kinds of white rice grain – long, medium and short. Brown rice is available in long and short grain. It can substitute for white rice in the following recipes, but should be cooked for 40–45 minutes. The long slender grains are fluffy and separate when cooked so are ideal for made-up savoury dishes and as an accompaniment to curries and stews. Medium and short grain rice have moister, stickier grains. The medium grains are suitable for savoury dishes where the rice is moulded or bound together. Short grain rice is used for sweet rice dishes.

BOILED RICE

Serves 3–4

225 g (8 oz) long grain white rice

5 ml (1 level tsp) salt

Place rice in a saucepan with 600 ml (1 pint) water and salt. Bring quickly to the boil, stir well and cover with a tightly fitting lid ■ Reduce the heat and simmer gently for 14–15 minutes. Remove from the heat and before serving separate out the grains gently, using a fork. (The rice will not need draining.)

CHICKEN RISOTTO

Serves 4

75 g (3 oz) butter or margarine
2 small onions, skinned and finely chopped
1 stick celery, washed, trimmed and chopped
1 green pepper, seeded and finely chopped
50 g (2 oz) mushrooms, sliced
1 garlic clove, skinned and crushed (optional)

50 g (2 oz) bacon or ham, chopped
225 g (8 oz) long grain white rice
600 ml (1 pint) chicken stock
chopped fresh herbs as available
salt and pepper
350 g (12 oz) cooked chicken, cut into strips
grated Parmesan cheese

Melt 50 g (2 oz) butter or margarine and add the chopped onion. Fry gently until softened. Add the celery, pepper, mushrooms and garlic if used, and the bacon or ham; fry for a further few minutes, stirring all the time ■ Add the rice and continue frying, stirring, until the rice is transparent ■ Add the stock, herbs, salt and pepper. Bring to the boil, cover and simmer for 10 minutes. Add the chicken strips and stir well ■ Continue cooking until the rice has absorbed the liquid. Stir in the remaining butter and some Parmesan cheese and serve.

STUFFED PEPPERS

Serves 4

4 green peppers
40 g (1½ oz) butter or
  margarine
1 onion, skinned and
  chopped
4 tomatoes, skinned and
  chopped
100 g (4 oz) bacon, rinded
  and chopped

100 g (4 oz) long grain
  rice, cooked
salt and pepper
50 g (2 oz) Cheddar
  cheese, grated
25 g (1 oz) fresh
  breadcrumbs
150 ml (¼ pint) stock

Wipe the peppers and cut off the ends 1 cm (½ inch) below the stalk. Scoop out the seeds and core with a knife, then wash out the cases and stand them up in an ovenproof dish ■ Heat 25 g (1 oz) butter and lightly fry the onion and tomatoes; add the bacon and fry lightly. Add the cooked rice and seasoning and half the grated cheese ■ Mix the rest of the cheese with the breadcrumbs. Put the rice stuffing into the pepper cases and sprinkle with the breadcrumb mixture ■ Pour the stock round the base of the cases and cook in the oven at 190°C (375°F) mark 5 for 15–20 minutes, or until the pepper cases are cooked.

Scooping out seeds

Putting stuffing in cases

PASTA

Pasta is available plain, wholewheat, spinach (verdi), tomato, basil and garlic and can be bought fresh, raw, dried or pre-cooked dried in a variety of different shapes. The most common are described here:

Spaghetti is a thin solid rod in lengths of either 25.5 cm (10 inches) or 51 cm (20 inches). Lower it into boiling salted water and, as it softens, curve it into the pan without breaking the pieces.

Macaroni is much thicker than spaghetti and has a hole through the middle. It comes in long rods like spaghetti, or as shortcut macaroni in pieces about 2.5–4 cm (1–1½ inches) long.

Lasagne comes in flat strips 5 cm (2 inches) or 10 cm (4 inches) wide. It may be plain or green, which is flavoured with spinach.

Long noodles are narrow flat pasta in rods the same lengths as spaghetti.

Cannelloni are large tubes about 10 cm (4 inches) long, served stuffed with savoury mixtures.

Spirals, shells and other shapes are also available.

To cook pasta

Allow 50–75 g (2–3 oz) per person as an accompaniment, whatever the shape. Put the pasta in a large saucepan of fast boiling water with 5 ml (1 level tsp) salt and cook uncovered for 10–15 minutes, until the pasta is tender but still has some 'bite' in it. Drain thoroughly.

PASTA

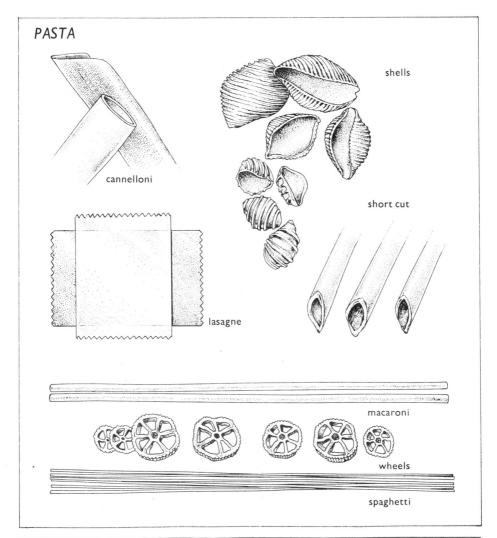

cannelloni

shells

short cut

lasagne

macaroni

wheels

spaghetti

SPAGHETTI BOLOGNESE

Serves 4

30 ml (2 tbsp) vegetable oil
1 medium onion, skinned and chopped
1 carrot, peeled and sliced
50 g (2 oz) bacon, rinded and chopped
450 g (1 lb) minced beef
226-g (8-oz) can tomatoes

50 g (2 oz) mushrooms, sliced
salt and pepper
a good dash of Worcestershire sauce
10 ml (2 level tsp) sugar
30 ml (2 tbsp) white wine or beer
350 g (12 oz) spaghetti

Winding spaghetti into pan

Put a large pan of salted water on to boil ■ Heat the oil in a large frying pan and lightly fry the onion, carrot and bacon. Add the minced beef and fry until well browned. Add the tomatoes and mushrooms, then the seasonings and wine, and simmer for 15–20 minutes ■ Wind the spaghetti into the pan of boiling water and boil for 10–12 minutes ■ When the spaghetti is cooked, drain and arrange on a dish ■ Pour the meat sauce over the spaghetti.

Note: The canned tomatoes may be replaced by 350 g ($\frac{3}{4}$ lb) fresh tomatoes, skinned and chopped, or 30 ml (2 tbsp) tomato purée.

PASTA NIÇOISE

Serves 2

100 g (4 oz) pasta spirals
2 eggs, hard-boiled and shelled
113-g (4-oz) can tuna fish, drained and flaked
2 firm tomatoes, quartered
$\frac{1}{2}$ red pepper, seeded and finely sliced

50 g (2 oz) French beans, cooked
8 black olives
few capers
45 ml (3 tbsp) garlic flavoured French dressing (see page 68)

Cook the pasta in boiling salted water for about 10 minutes until tender but not soft. Drain well and rinse at once in cold water. Cool ■ Quarter the hard-boiled eggs. Place the pasta, fish, tomatoes, red pepper, beans, olives and capers in a bowl and mix gently ■ Add French dressing and toss, using two forks. Spoon on to a serving dish or 2 individual plates. Garnish with the quartered hard-boiled eggs.

SPAGHETTI ALLA CARBONARA

Serves 4

350 g (12 oz) spaghetti
salt
2 eggs
2 egg yolks
90 ml (6 level tbsp) grated Parmesan cheese
75 g (3 oz) Cheddar cheese, grated
225 g (8 oz) streaky bacon, rinded

6 tomatoes, skinned, seeded and chopped
150 ml ($\frac{1}{4}$ pint) single cream
30 ml (2 tbsp) chopped fresh parsley
50 g (2 oz) butter or margarine
freshly ground black pepper

Cook the spaghetti in fast boiling salted water for about 10–15 minutes until tender but not soft. Drain well ■ Beat together the eggs and egg yolks, stir in half the Parmesan and half the Cheddar and set aside ■ Snip the bacon with scissors and fry without any extra fat until crisp. Stir in the chopped tomato ■ Reduce the heat and add the cream and parsley. Allow to simmer while the spaghetti is cooking ■ Soften the butter in the spaghetti saucepan and return the spaghetti to it. Add the bacon and cream mixture and toss well, using 2 forks. Finally add the egg mixture; toss well again. (The heat of the spaghetti is sufficient to cook the eggs.) ■ Adjust the seasoning and turn the mixture into a heated serving dish. Sprinkle the remaining cheeses on top.

Draining spaghetti

Adding egg mixture

MACARONI CHEESE

Serves 4

175 g (6 oz) shortcut macaroni
40 g (1½ oz) butter or margarine
60 ml (4 level tbsp) plain flour

568 ml (1 pint) milk
175 g (6 oz) Cheddar cheese, grated
salt, pepper and mustard
1 tomato, sliced

Grease an ovenproof dish. Half-fill a large saucepan with water, bring to the boil and add 10 ml (2 level tsp) salt. Drop in the macaroni and cook rapidly for 10 minutes; drain well ■ Meanwhile melt the fat, stir in the flour and cook for 2–3 minutes. Remove the pan from the heat and gradually stir in the milk. Bring to the boil and continue to stir until the sauce thickens; remove from the heat and add the cheese, saving 30–45 ml (2–3 tbsp) for the topping. Season to taste with salt, pepper and mustard ■ Add the cooked macaroni to the cheese sauce and mix thoroughly. Put into the dish and sprinkle with the remaining cheese. Arrange the tomato on the top and put under a hot grill until the cheese is golden.

LASAGNE AL FORNO

Serves 4

two 396-g (14-oz) cans
  tomatoes
63-g (2¼-oz) can tomato
  purée
2.5–5 ml (½–1 level tsp)
  dried marjoram
salt and pepper
5 ml (1 level tsp) sugar
225 g (8 oz) cooked ham,
  diced

100 g (4 oz) lasagne
175 g (6 oz) ricotta or
  curd cheese (or a blend
  of half cottage cheese
  and half full fat soft
  cheese)
50 g (2 oz) grated
  Parmesan cheese
225 g (8 oz) Mozzarella or
  Bel Paese cheese

Combine the canned tomatoes, tomato purée, marjoram, seasoning and sugar, simmer gently for about 30 minutes and add the ham ■ Cook the lasagne for 10–15 minutes in boiling salted water (or as stated on the packet) and drain well ■ Cover the base of a fairly deep ovenproof dish with a layer of the tomato and meat sauce. Add half the lasagne, put in another layer of the sauce, then cover with the cheeses, using half of each kind ■ Repeat these layers with the remaining ingredients, finishing with a layer of cheese. Bake in the oven at 190°C (375°F) mark 5 for 30 minutes, until golden and bubbling on top.

Adding first layer of sauce

Adding half the lasagne

STUFFED BAKED APPLES

Serves 4

4 even-sized cooking
  apples
75–100 g (3–4 oz) mixed
  dried fruit
30 ml (2 level tbsp)
  demerara sugar

knob of butter or
  margarine
30 ml (2 tbsp) water

Remove the centres from the apples with a corer and make a cut in the skin round the middle of each apple ■ Put them in an ovenproof dish. Fill the holes with the mixed fruit and sugar. Put a knob of butter on each apple and pour the water round them ■ Bake in the oven at 200°C (400°F) mark 6 for ~~¾~~ hour, until the apples are soft.

½

Removing centre from apples

Making cut in skin

VARIATIONS

1 Replace the demerara sugar with golden syrup, honey or white sugar.
2 Include marmalade, mincemeat, chopped dates, almonds, walnuts or crystallised ginger in the filling.
3 When the apples are cooked, remove the skin above the cut and cover them with a meringue mixture made from 2 egg whites and 100 g (4 oz) caster sugar. Replace in the oven until lightly browned.

RHUBARB CRUMBLE

Serves 4

450 g (1 lb) rhubarb
175 g (6 oz) sugar
75 g (3 oz) butter or
  margarine

175 g (6 oz) plain flour
15 ml (1 level tbsp)
  demerara sugar for
  topping

Cut the rhubarb into pieces and put in an ovenproof dish; add 75 g (3 oz) of the sugar ■ Rub the fat into the flour until the texture resembles breadcrumbs. Add the remaining sugar and mix together; sprinkle on top of the rhubarb. Finally sprinkle on the demerara sugar and bake in the oven at 180°C (350°F) mark 4 for 40–45 minutes ■ If you are using a soft fruit, or one that has been already stewed, cook the crumble at 190°C (375°F) mark 5 for about 20 minutes.

PANCAKES

Serves 4

125 g (4 oz) plain flour
a pinch of salt
1 egg
300 ml (½ pint) milk and
    water, mixed

a little lard
caster sugar
1 lemon, cut into wedges

Mix the flour and salt, make a well in the centre and break in the egg. Add half the liquid, gradually work in the flour using a wooden spoon and beat until the mixture is smooth. Add the remaining liquid gradually and beat until well mixed and the surface is covered with tiny bubbles ■ Melt just enough lard in a thick frying pan to coat the bottom and sides, then pour off any surplus. When the fat is hot, pour in a little batter – just enough to cover the bottom of the pan ■ Cook the pancake until it is golden brown on the underside, then toss or turn it over and cook the other side ■ Turn out on to a plate, sprinkle with sugar, cover with another plate and keep warm whilst the rest are being made ■ When all the pancakes are cooked roll them up singly and serve with wedges of lemon.

Turning pancake

Serving

APPLE PIE

Serves 4

200 g (7 oz) shortcrust
    pastry (see page 104)
450 g (1 lb) cooking
    apples, peeled and
    sliced

100 g (4 oz) demerara
    sugar
4 cloves
egg or milk to glaze

Lining bottom of pie plate

Putting on lid

Roll out half the pastry and line the bottom of an 18-cm (7-inch) pie plate ■ Fill the plate with the sliced apples, sprinkle with the sugar and add the cloves ■ Roll out the remaining half of the pastry to make the top crust of the pie. Brush the edge of the bottom layer of pastry with water, put on the lid and seal well. Mark the edges with a knife and crimp together. Brush with beaten egg or milk ■ Bake in the oven at 200°C (400°F) mark 6 for 15–20 minutes, then lower the temperature to 180°C (350°F) mark 4 and cook for a further 15–20 minutes, or until the apple is cooked (test with a thin skewer).

BANANAS WITH HONEY AND ORANGE

Serves 4

25 g (1 oz) butter
45 ml (3 tbsp) clear honey
2.5 ml (½ level tsp) mixed
  spice

grated rind of 1 orange
juice of 2 oranges
4 medium bananas, peeled
  and halved lengthways

Melt the butter and honey in a large frying pan and add the spice, orange rind and juice ■ Place the banana slices in the syrup and gently poach for 5 minutes ■ Serve hot with whipped cream.

BAKED JAM SPONGE

Serves 3–4

75 g (3 oz) butter or
  margarine
75 g (3 oz) caster sugar
1 egg, beaten
150 g (5 oz) self raising
  flour

2.5 ml (½ tsp) vanilla
  flavouring
milk to mix
30–45 ml (2–3 tbsp) jam

Grease a 600–900-ml (1–1½-pint) pie dish ■ Cream the fat and sugar until pale and fluffy. Add the egg a little at a time, beating after each addition. Fold in the flour with the flavouring and a little milk to give a dropping consistency ■ Put the jam in a layer in the base of the prepared dish and spoon in the sponge mixture ■ Bake in the oven at 180°C (350°F) mark 4 for 30–40 minutes, until well risen and golden. Serve with a custard sauce.

Creaming fat and sugar

Putting jam in dish

LEMON MERINGUE PIE

Serves 4

shortcrust pastry made
  with 150 g (5 oz) flour
  (see page 104)
45 ml (3 level tbsp)
  cornflour
150 ml (¼ pint) water
juice and grated rind of
  2 lemons

100 g (4 oz) sugar
2 eggs, separated
75 g (3 oz) caster sugar
glacé cherries and
  angelica

Roll out the pastry and use it to line an 18-cm (7-inch) flan case or deep pie plate. Trim the edges and bake blind (see page 106) in the oven at 220°C (425°F) mark 7 for 15 minutes. Remove the paper and baking beans and return the case to the oven for a further 5 minutes. Reduce the oven temperature to 180°C (350°F) mark 4 ■ Mix the cornflour with the water in a saucepan, add the lemon juice and rind and bring slowly to the boil, stirring until the mixture thickens, then add the sugar. Remove from the heat, cool the mixture slightly and add the egg yolks. Pour into the pastry case ■ Whisk the egg whites until stiff, whisk in half the caster sugar and fold in the rest. Pile the meringue on top of the lemon filling and bake in the oven for about 10 minutes, or until the meringue is crisp and lightly browned. Decorate before serving with cherries and angelica.

Stirring until mixture thickens

Whisking in half sugar

Spooning meringue on filling

CHRISTMAS PUDDINGS

175 g (6 oz) almonds
550 g (1¼ lb) stoned
  raisins
350 g (12 oz) currants
225 g (8 oz) sultanas
100 g (4 oz) mixed peel
100 g (4 oz) glacé cherries
225 g (8 oz) apples, peeled
  and cored
grated rind and juice of
  1 lemon and 1 orange
350 g (12 oz) plain flour
5 ml (1 level tsp) salt

10 ml (2 level tsp) mixed
  spice
350 g (12 oz) fresh
  breadcrumbs
350 g (12 oz) shredded
  suet
225 g (8 oz) caster sugar
225 g (8 oz) soft brown
  sugar
60 ml (4 tbsp) brandy
4 eggs
about 150 ml (¼ pint) milk

Grease 3 pudding basins – 600-ml, 900-ml, 1.1-litre (1-pint, 1½-pint and 2-pint). Blanch the almonds, remove the skins when cool, then dry the nuts. Wash and dry the fruit thoroughly, or rub it in flour on a sieve to remove any small stalks, etc. Chop the nuts, peel, cherries and apple and mix with the diced fruit and the lemon and orange rind. Add the mixture to the flour, salt, spice, breadcrumbs, suet and sugars ■ Mix together the fruit juices, brandy and eggs and mix very thoroughly with the dry ingredients, adding enough milk to give a dropping consistency ■ Turn the mixture into the prepared basins and cover with greaseproof paper and a pudding cloth or foil secured with string. Either steam or boil in a saucepan with water coming halfway up the basins. Allow the following times:

600-ml (1-pint) pudding – about 5 hours
900-ml (1½-pint) pudding – about 7 hours
1.1-litre (2-pint) pudding – about 9 hours

When the puddings are cool, remove the pudding cloths and replace with new ones ■ The puddings will keep for 4 months. Before serving, cook again for the following times:

600-ml (1-pint) pudding – 2 hours
900-ml (1½-pint) pudding – 3 hours
1.1-litre (2-pint) pudding – 3 hours.

Removing skins from almonds

Rubbing fruit in flour

Grating lemon

Securing pudding cloth

STEWED PLUMS

Serves 4

450 g (1 lb) plums
75–100 g (3–4 oz) sugar

300 ml (½ pint) water

Halve and stone the plums, reserving the stones. Crack the stones with nutcrackers and remove the kernels; reserve ■ Make a syrup by dissolving the sugar in the water over a gentle heat. Add the plums and the kernels and simmer gently until the fruit is soft but keeps its shape ■ Remove the kernels with a slotted spoon before serving.

MINCE PIES

Makes about 20

Filling with mincemeat

shortcrust pastry made
 with 350 g (12 oz) flour
 (see page 104)
350–450 g ($\frac{3}{4}$–1 lb)
 mincemeat

milk or egg to glaze
caster sugar for dusting

Roll out the pastry to about 0.3 cm ($\frac{1}{8}$ inch) thick. Cut into about 20 rounds with a 7.5-cm (3-inch) fluted cutter and 20 smaller rounds with a 5.5-cm (2$\frac{1}{4}$-inch) cutter ■ Line 6.5-cm (2$\frac{1}{2}$-inch) patty tins with the larger rounds and fill with mincemeat. Damp the edges of the small rounds and place firmly in position on top of the pies ■ Make a small slit in the top of each pie, brush with milk or egg and bake in the oven at 220°C (425°F) mark 7 for 15–20 minutes, until light golden brown. Cool on a wire rack ■ Reheat and dust with caster sugar before serving.

APPLE AND BLACKBERRY CHARLOTTE

Serves 4

450 g (1 lb) cooking
 apples, peeled
450 g (1 lb) blackberries
grated rind and juice of
 $\frac{1}{2}$ a lemon
1.25 ml ($\frac{1}{4}$ level tsp)
 ground cinnamon

50 g (2 oz) butter, melted
6 slices bread from a large
 white loaf, crusts
 removed
175–225 g (6–8 oz) sugar
30 ml (2 level tbsp) bread
 or cake crumbs

Quarter the apples and remove the cores; wash and pick over the blackberries. Stew the fruit in a pan with the lemon rind and juice and the cinnamon ■ Brush a charlotte mould or a 12.5-cm (5-inch) cake tin generously with melted butter ■ Trim one piece of bread to a round the same size as the base of the tin, dip it into melted butter and fit it into the bottom of the tin. Dip the remaining slices of bread in the butter and arrange closely around the sides of the tin, reserving one piece for the top ■ Add the sugar and crumbs to the stewed fruit, mix well and fill the tin. Cover with the remaining slice of bread, trimmed to fit the top of the mould ■ Cook in the oven at 190°C (375°F) mark 5 for about 1 hour, turn out and serve with custard or cream.

Fitting bread in bottom of tin

Arranging slices round sides

Covering with slice of bread

COLD PUDDINGS

APRICOT FOOL

Serves 4

439-g (15½-oz) can
    apricots
150 ml (¼ pint) custard
150 ml (¼ pint) double
    cream

chopped walnuts
    (optional)

Drain the apricots and purée in a blender or rub through a sieve. Add this pulp to the custard. Lightly whip the cream and fold into the mixture. Pile into glasses and decorate the top with chopped nuts, if used.

Fruit fool is an adaptable sweet that can be made from many types of fruit, though those with a strong colour look best, eg rhubarb, damsons, raspberries, blackberries and perhaps the most traditional of all, gooseberries.
For a more economical version, use all custard – for parties, increase the proportion of cream; the authentic old English recipe uses all cream, giving a gorgeous rich sweet.
Serve something crisp with fruit fool as a contrast to its smooth texture – for instance, plain sweet biscuits or sponge fingers.

RASPBERRY MOUSSE

Serves 4

450 g (1 lb) raspberries,
    or two 425-g (15-oz)
    cans raspberries,
    drained
caster sugar to taste
150 ml (¼ pint) double
    or whipping cream,
    whipped

20 ml (4 level tsp) gelatine
45 ml (3 tbsp) water or
    juice from the canned
    raspberries
2 egg whites
whipped cream to
    decorate

Sieve the raspberries, to make about 300 ml (½ pint) purée. Stir in sugar to taste and the whipped cream. Put the water or fruit juice in a small basin and sprinkle the gelatine on it, stand the basin in a pan of hot water and heat gently until the gelatine is dissolved; allow to cool slightly ■ Pour the gelatine into the raspberry cream in a steady stream, stirring the mixture all the time ■ Whisk the egg whites until stiff and fold them into the raspberry cream, using a large metal spoon. Pour the mousse into a serving dish and chill until set. Decorate with whipped cream before serving.

CHOCOLATE MOUSSE

Serves 4

175 g (6 oz) plain chocolate
3 eggs, separated
150 ml ($\frac{1}{4}$ pint) double cream, whipped

grated chocolate or finely chopped nuts

Melt the chocolate in a bowl over a pan of hot water. Remove from the heat then beat the yolks into the melted chocolate ■ Whisk the whites until stiff and carefully fold into the chocolate mixture ■ Chill and serve in individual ramekin dishes or small sundae glasses, topped with whipped cream and grated chocolate or chopped nuts.

TO MELT CHOCOLATE
Break up the chocolate and place the pieces into a heatproof bowl which will fit over a saucepan. Half fill the saucepan with water and stand over a low heat. Stir the chocolate until it melts.

FRUIT TRIFLE

Serves 4

6 individual sponge cakes
raspberry jam
1 glass sherry or fruit juice
2 bananas, sliced

2 peaches, sliced
450 ml ($\frac{3}{4}$ pint) custard
150 ml ($\frac{1}{4}$ pint) double cream
chocolate vermicelli

Split the sponge cakes, spread with jam, cut into small pieces and place in the bottom of a large bowl ■ Pour the sherry or fruit juice over and leave to soak for 30 minutes ■ Cover the cake with the mixed fruits. Pour the custard over the cake and fruit and allow to set ■ Whip the cream lightly, spread over the top and sprinkle chocolate vermicelli round the edge.

FRUIT FLANS

shortcrust flan case, baked blind (see page 106)

For fresh fruit filling
225 g (8 oz) fresh fruit, eg raspberries, strawberries
30–35 ml (2–3 tbsp) redcurrant jelly or $\frac{1}{2}$ packet red jelly

For canned fruit filling
425-g (15-oz) can fruit
15 ml (1 level tbsp) cornflour
150 ml ($\frac{1}{4}$ pint) fruit juice

For a fresh fruit flan, pick over the fruit, wash it and arrange in the flan case ■ Make a glaze by melting the redcurrant jelly with about 15 ml (1 tbsp) water or by making up the table jelly. When it begins to thicken, brush the glaze over the fruit. Leave to set before serving ▪ For a canned fruit flan, arrange the drained fruit in the flan case, filling it well. Blend the cornflour with a little of the fruit juice to a smooth cream. Boil the rest of the juice and stir into the blended cornflour. Return this mixture to the pan and bring to the boil, stirring until a thickened glaze is obtained. Spoon over the fruit to coat it evenly ▪ In each case, adapt the quantity of fruit to suit the size of the flan case.

LEMON CHEESECAKE

Serves 8

1½ packets of lemon jelly
60 ml (4 tbsp) water
2 eggs, separated
300 ml (½ pint) milk
grated rind of 2 lemons
90 ml (6 tbsp) lemon juice
450 g (1 lb) cottage cheese
15 ml (1 level tbsp) caster sugar
150 ml (¼ pint) double cream, whipped

glacé cherries and mint sprigs

For the crumb base
100 g (4 oz) digestive biscuits
50 g (2 oz) caster sugar
50 g (2 oz) butter or margarine, melted

Put the jelly and water in a small pan and warm gently over a low heat, stirring until dissolved ▪ Beat together the egg yolks and milk, pour on to the jelly, stir and return the mixture to the heat for a few minutes without boiling. Remove from the heat and add the lemon rind and juice ▪ Sieve the cottage cheese and stir it into the jelly, or put both jelly and cottage cheese in a blender and purée until smooth. Turn the mixture into a bowl ▪ Whisk the egg whites until stiff, add the caster sugar and whisk again until stiff; fold into the cheese mixture. Fold in the whipped cream and spoon the mixture into a 20.5-cm (8-inch) spring release cake tin fitted with a tube base ▪ Crush the biscuits and stir in the sugar and butter. Use to cover the cheese mixture, pressing it on lightly; chill ▪ Turn the cheesecake out carefully and decorate with cherries and mint sprigs.

Sieving cottage cheese

Crushing biscuits

Covering cheese mixture

Turning out cheesecake

SUMMER PUDDING

Serves 4

150 g (5 oz) sugar
30 ml (2 tbsp) water
450 g (1 lb) mixed
blackcurrants, stringed
and washed, and
raspberries, washed

100–175 g (4–6 oz) white
bread, cut in thin slices
whipped cream or custard

Stir the sugar and water together in a saucepan and bring slowly to the boil. Add the fruits and stew gently until they are soft but retain their shape ■ Cut the crusts from the bread and line a 900-ml (1½-pint) pudding basin with the slices ■ Pour in the fruit and cover with more slices of bread. Place a saucer with a weight on it on top of the pudding and leave overnight in a cool place ■ Turn out the pudding and serve with whipped cream or custard ■ Other soft fruits (or a mixture) may be used in summer pudding, providing they have a rich, strong colour – for example raspberries, redcurrants, damsons. A proportion of apple can also be included.

Lining pudding basin with bread

Weighting down pudding

Turning out pudding

STRAWBERRY SHORTCAKE

Serves 4–6

225 g (8 oz) self raising
flour
pinch of salt
100 g (4 oz) butter or
margarine
75 g (3 oz) sugar
1 egg, beaten

15–30 ml (1–2 tbsp) milk
350–450 g (¾–1 lb)
strawberries
45–60 ml (3–4 level tbsp)
caster sugar
150 ml (¼ pint) double
cream

Grease a 20.5-cm (8-inch) sandwich cake tin ■ Sift the flour and salt together and rub in the fat until the mixture resembles breadcrumbs; stir in the sugar. Add the egg a little at a time and a little milk, so that the mixture begins to stick together ■ Collect the mixture together with the hand and knead lightly into a smooth, fairly firm dough. Turn on to a floured board and roll out the dough into a round 20.5 cm (8 inches) across ■ Press the dough evenly into the cake tin and bake in the oven at 190°C (375°F) mark 5 for 20 minutes, or until golden and firm. Turn out

of the tin on to a cooling tray ■ Wash the strawberries and remove the hulls and stems. Keep about
a dozen berries for decorating; lightly crush the rest
and sprinkle with 30–45 ml (2–3 tbsp) sugar ■ Split
the shortcake, spread the lower half with the crushed
fruit and replace the top. Add the remaining sugar to
the cream and pile on the cake. Decorate with the
whole berries.

Rolling out dough

Splitting shortcake   ·

Decorating with whole berries

ORANGE WATER ICE

Serves 4

100 g (4 oz) caster sugar
300 ml (½ pint) water
15 ml (1 tbsp) lemon juice
grated rind of 1 orange
*   and 1 lemon*

juice of 3 oranges and
*   1 lemon mixed, about*
*   300 ml (½ pint)*
1 egg white

Set the refrigerator to the coldest setting ■ Dissolve the sugar in the water over a low heat, bring to
the boil and boil gently for 10 minutes. Add 15 ml
(1 tbsp) lemon juice ■ Put the grated rinds in a
basin, pour the boiling syrup over and leave until
cold ■ Add the mixed fruit juices, strain into a
freezing tray and place in the freezing compartment
of the refrigerator ■ Leave until half-frozen, then
turn the mixture into a bowl ■ Whisk the egg
white until stiff then fold into the frozen mixture.
Return to the tray and freeze ■ Other flavours of
water ices (eg raspberry, strawberry) can be made
by adding 300 ml (½ pint) fruit purée and the juice of
½ a lemon to 300 ml (½ pint) of the syrup; continue
as above.

FRUIT SORBET

Follow the water ice recipe but add twice the amount
of egg white, which will give a much softer consistency. Freeze the mixture in the freezing compartment of the refrigerator with the control at the
normal setting, until the sorbet is sufficiently stiff for
serving; spoon it into glasses.

FRUIT SALAD

Serves 4

220-g (7¾-oz) can pineapple chunks
100–175 g (4–6 oz) sugar
2 bananas, peeled
2 red eating apples

1 orange, skinned
1 pear, peeled
50 g (2 oz) black or white grapes

Open the can of pineapple, strain off the juice and make up to 300 ml (½ pint) with water. Place this with the sugar in a saucepan and heat slowly to dissolve the sugar; cool for a moment and pour into a glass bowl ■ Add all the fruits to the bowl, preparing them as necessary; slice the bananas; cut the apples into quarters, remove the cores and cut into thin slices; slice the skinned orange across; cut the pear into thin slices; cut the grapes in half and remove the pips ■ Mix all together and leave to stand for a time before serving ■ Cream or ice cream is often served with a fruit salad.

CRÈME CARAMEL

Serves 4–6

115 g (4½ oz) sugar
150 ml (¼ pint) water

568 ml (1 pint) milk
4 eggs

Put 100 g (4 oz) of the sugar and the water into a small pan and dissolve the sugar slowly; bring to the boil and boil without stirring until it caramelises, ie becomes a rich golden brown ■ Pour the caramel into a 15-cm (6-inch) cake tin which has been heated slightly, turning the tin until the bottom is completely covered ■ Warm the milk, pour on to the lightly whisked eggs and remaining sugar and strain over the cooled caramel ■ Place the tin in a shallow tin of water and bake in the oven at 170°C (325°F) mark 3 for 1 hour, until set ■ Leave in the tin until quite cold (preferably until the next day) before turning out ■ Individual crèmes are easier to turn out. Divide the mixture between six 150-ml (¼-pint) caramel coated tins. Cook for about 45 minutes.

Pouring on milk

Placing tin in tin of water

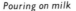

ICE CREAM

Serves 4

150 ml (¼ pint) double
cream or chilled
evaporated milk
150 ml (¼ pint) vanilla-
flavoured custard

sweetened with
45–60 ml (3–4 tbsp)
caster sugar

Set the refrigerator to the coldest setting. Whisk the cream or evaporated milk until it is thick and will hold a 'trail' ■ Fold into the cool custard, turn the mixture into a freezing tray and place in the refrigerator ■ When the ice cream has started to freeze (about 1 hour, depending on the refrigerator) turn it out from the tray into a bowl and whisk again. Return it to the ice tray and freeze until required ■ Spoon into glasses and serve with fruit or a sauce.

Whisking cream until thick

Turning mixture into freezing tray

VARIATIONS

Chocolate – add 40 g (1½ oz) melted chocolate.
Coffee – add 10 ml (2 level tsp) powdered or granulated coffee dissolved in 5 ml (1 tsp) hot water.
Banana – add 2 small bananas, puréed or mashed.
Ginger – add 40 g (1½ oz) preserved ginger (chopped) and 5 ml (1 tsp) ginger syrup.

SAUCES, STUFFINGS AND ACCOMPANIMENTS

WHITE SAUCE

20 g (¾ oz) butter or margarine
30 ml (2 level tbsp) plain flour

300 ml (½ pint) milk
salt and pepper

Melt the fat in a small saucepan, add the flour and stir well with a wooden spoon until smooth. Cook for 2–3 minutes then remove it from the heat ■ Add the milk a little at a time, stirring thoroughly before adding any more. Return the sauce to the heat and bring to the boil, stirring all the time, until it thickens. Cook for a further 1–2 minutes. Season to taste ■ For a coating sauce use 25 g (1 oz) each of fat and flour to 300 ml (½ pint) milk.

Melting fat in saucepan

Adding flour and stirring

Adding milk

VARIATIONS

Use a base of 300 ml (½ pint) white sauce.

Parsley Add 30 ml (2 tbsp) chopped parsley. If the sauce is to accompany fish, add a little lemon juice or vinegar; stir thoroughly and reheat.

Cheese To the hot sauce add 50–75 g (2–3 oz) grated cheese, a little mustard and a few drops of Worcestershire sauce.

Onion Skin and chop 1–2 onions and cook in just enough water to cover until tender. Use 150 ml (¼ pint) cooking liquid and 150 ml (¼ pint) milk to make the sauce, then add the onion.

Egg Add 1–2 finely chopped hard-boiled eggs.

Anchovy Omit the salt. Add 15–30 ml (1–2 tbsp) anchovy essence to taste and a drop or two of pink colouring to tint.

Mushroom Add 50 g (2 oz) sliced sautéd button mushrooms and cook for 2–3 minutes.

Shrimp Add 25–50 g (1–2 oz) chopped shrimps (or prawns), with a little lemon juice and anchovy essence.

Caper Add 25–50 g (1–2 oz) capers (chopped or whole) and a little of the liquid or some lemon juice.

BREAD SAUCE

a few cloves
1 onion, skinned
450 ml (¾ pint) milk
75 g (3 oz) fresh
breadcrumbs

knob of butter
salt and pepper

Stick the cloves into the onion, put in a saucepan with the milk and bring almost to the boil; leave for 20 minutes ■ Add the crumbs and butter and season to taste. Remove the onion and reheat.

MINT SAUCE

small bunch of fresh mint
10 ml (2 level tsp) sugar
15 ml (1 tbsp) boiling
water

30 ml (2 tbsp) vinegar

Wash the mint and strip the leaves from the stalks; chop as finely as possible ■ Put the sugar into a sauceboat, pour on the boiling water, stir until dissolved, then add the chopped mint and vinegar.

Chopping mint finely   *Adding vinegar*

GRAVY

A rich brown gravy is served with all roast joints. There should be no need to use extra colouring or flavouring if the gravy is properly made in the baking tin after the joint has been removed.

To make thin gravy, pour the fat very slowly from the tin, draining it off carefully from one corner and leaving the sediment behind. Season well with salt and pepper and add 300 ml ($\frac{1}{2}$ pint) hot vegetable water or stock (which can be made from a bouillon cube). Stir thoroughly until all the sediment is scraped from the tin and the gravy is a rich brown; return the pan to the heat and boil for 2–3 minutes. Serve very hot.

To make a thick gravy, leave 30 ml (2 tbsp) of the fat in the tin, add 30 ml (2 level tbsp) flour (if this is shaken from a flour dredger it gives a smoother result), blend well and cook over the heat until it turns brown, stirring continuously. Carefully mix in 300 ml ($\frac{1}{2}$ pint) hot stock, boil for 2–3 minutes, season well, strain and serve very hot.

Greasy gravy, due to not draining off enough fat, or thin gravy, due to adding too much liquid, can be corrected by adding more flour, although this weakens the flavour. If the sauce is very pale, extra colouring can be added in the form of gravy browning. Meat extracts, which are sometimes added to give extra taste, overpower the characteristic meat flavour. However, a sliced carrot and onion cooked with the joint in the gravy will give extra 'body' to the taste without impairing it; 15 ml (1 tbsp) cider or wine added at the last moment does wonders.

BARBECUE SAUCE

Serves 4

50 g (2 oz) butter
1 large onion, skinned and chopped
5 ml (1 level tsp) tomato purée
30 ml (2 tbsp) vinegar
30 ml (2 level tbsp) demerara sugar

10 ml (2 level tsp) dry mustard
30 ml (2 tbsp) Worcestershire sauce
150 ml ($\frac{1}{4}$ pint) water

Melt the butter and fry the onion for 5 minutes or until soft. Stir in the tomato purée and continue cooking for a further 3 minutes ■ Blend the remaining ingredients to a smooth cream and stir in the onion mixture ■ Return the sauce to the pan and simmer uncovered for a further 10 minutes ■ Serve with chicken, sausages, hamburgers or chops.

TOMATO SAUCE

Makes about
450 ml (¾ pint)

½ onion, skinned and
  chopped
2 rashers of bacon, rinded
  and chopped
knob of butter
25 ml (1½ level tbsp) plain
  flour
396-g (14-oz) can
  tomatoes

1 clove
½ bay leaf
few sprigs of rosemary, or
  5 ml (1 level tsp) dried
  mixed herbs
pinch of sugar
salt and pepper

Fry the onion and bacon gently in the butter for
5 minutes ■ Stir in the flour and gradually add
the tomatoes with their juice, also the flavourings
and seasoning ■ Simmer gently for 15 minutes,
then sieve and if necessary reseason ■ Serve with
croquettes, pasta and other savoury dishes.

EGG CUSTARD SAUCE

Makes about
300 ml (½ pint)

1½ eggs or 3 yolks
15 ml (1 level tbsp) sugar
300 ml (½ pint) milk

few strips of thinly pared
  lemon rind or ½ vanilla
  pod, split

Whisk the eggs or yolks and sugar lightly. Warm
the milk and lemon rind or vanilla pod and leave for
10 minutes for the flavour to infuse ■ Pour the
milk on to the eggs then strain the mixture into
the top of a double saucepan or into a thick based
saucepan. Stir over a very gentle heat until the sauce
thickens and lightly coats the back of the spoon. Do
not let it boil or it will curdle ■ Serve hot or cold
with fruit sweets and puddings.

Pouring the milk on to the eggs

BRANDY BUTTER

75 g (3 oz) butter
75 g (3 oz) caster sugar

10–15 ml (2–3 tsp)
  brandy

Cream the butter until pale and soft. Beat in the
sugar gradually, then add the brandy a few drops at a
time, taking care not to allow the mixture to curdle.
The finished sauce should be pale and frothy. Pile it
into a small dish and leave to harden before serving
with Christmas pudding.

APPLE SAUCE

Serves 4

450 g (1 lb) cooking
  apples, peeled and
  cored

25 g (1 oz) butter
little sugar

Slice the apples and simmer in an open saucepan with 30–45 ml (2–3 tbsp) water until soft and thick – about 10 minutes ▪ Beat to a pulp with a wooden spoon or potato masher then purée in a blender or rub through a sieve if you wish ▪ Stir in the butter and add a little sugar if the apples are very tart ▪ Serve with pork or sausages.

FORCEMEAT

100 g (4 oz) fresh
  breadcrumbs
25–50 g (1–2 oz) bacon or
  ham, chopped
15 ml (1 level tbsp)
  chopped fresh parsley

50 g (2 oz) suet
grated rind of $\frac{1}{4}$ a lemon
2.5 ml ($\frac{1}{2}$ level tsp) mixed
  herbs
salt and pepper
beaten egg

Mix all the ingredients together with a little beaten egg until the stuffing binds well ▪ Use with meat, poultry, fish and liver. Sufficient for an average-sized joint or chicken.

SAGE AND ONION STUFFING

2 large onions
25 g (1 oz) butter or
  margarine
100 g (4 oz) fresh
  breadcrumbs

10 ml (2 level tsp) dried
  sage
salt and pepper

Chop the onions finely, cook until tender in boiling salted water, then drain. Combine with the remaining ingredients and mix well ▪ Use with roast goose, duck and pork.

SAUSAGE STUFFING

1 large onion, skinned and
  chopped
450 g (1 lb) pork
  sausagemeat
25 g (1 oz) lard
10 ml (2 level tsp) chopped
  fresh parsley

5 ml (1 level tsp) mixed
  herbs
25 g (1 oz) fresh
  breadcrumbs (optional)
salt and pepper

Mix the onion with the sausagemeat. Melt the lard and fry the sausagemeat and onion lightly for 2–3 minutes. Add the rest of the ingredients and mix well ▪ Use with chicken and turkey. Sufficient for a 4–4.5 kg (9–10 lb) turkey.

YORKSHIRE PUDDING

Serves 4

125 g (4 oz) plain flour
pinch of salt
1 egg

300 ml (½ pint) milk and
water mixed

Sift the flour and salt into a mixing bowl and make a well in the centre. Pour the egg and 30 ml (2 tbsp) of the liquid into the well ▪ Using a wooden spoon and working from the centre, gradually mix some of the flour from the edges into the egg and milk and beat well until smooth ▪ Gradually add 150 ml (¼ pint) of the liquid, beating gently and drawing in the rest of the flour until all is mixed in and the batter is smooth and bubbly. Stir in the remaining liquid. Put a little lard or dripping into a shallow tin measuring about 18 cm (7 inches) square and heat in the oven. Pour in the batter and bake in the oven at 220°C (425°F) mark 7 for 40–45 minutes. Cut into squares and serve with roast beef.

Pouring egg and liquid in well   *Pouring batter in shallow tin*

POPOVERS

Makes about 12

Make the batter as for Yorkshire pudding. Heat the oven to 220°C (425°F) mark 7. Put a little lard or dripping into some patty tins, heat in the oven, then pour some batter into each tin. Bake near the top of the oven for 15–20 minutes. Serve with roast beef.

Pouring batter in patty tins

PASTRY

There is no room for guesswork in pastry-making –
the ingredients must be in the correct proportions
and mixed to the correct consistency. Cool working
conditions and a hot oven are usually essential and
the dough should be handled as little as possible –
over-kneading gives a tough, hard result.

Plain flour is usually recommended for making pastry;
if self raising is used, it gives a more open and spongy
texture. A variety of fats (including butter, margarine
and lard, or a combination) can be used for shortcrust, but for richer pastries it is better to use
the fat recommended in the particular recipe. Pro-
prietary vegetable shortenings are excellent; follow
the makers' directions, as they sometimes advise
using less fat to flour than in standard recipes.
Avoid using too much flour on board and rolling pin,
as this alters the proportions. Take care also with
the liquid – too much makes the pastry tough.

Note: '200 g (7 oz) pastry' means pastry made with
200 g (7 oz) flour and other ingredients in proportion.
With ready-made pastries, the amount means weight
as bought.

SHORTCRUST PASTRY

200 g (7 oz) plain flour
2.5 ml ($\frac{1}{2}$ level tsp) salt
100 g ($3\frac{1}{2}$ oz) fat, $\frac{1}{2}$ lard
  $\frac{1}{2}$ margarine

about 35 ml (7 tsp) cold
  water

Sift the flour and salt into a basin ■ Cut the fats
into the flour and complete the mixing by rubbing in
with the fingertips, until no lumps of fat remain ■
Add just enough cold water to bind the mixture,
mixing with a round-bladed knife until it is evenly
distributed ■ Draw the pastry together with the
fingertips to form a stiff dough; knead lightly until
smooth ■ Turn it on to a lightly floured board
and roll out and use as required.

Sifting flour and salt

Rubbing in with fingertips

Adding cold water

Drawing pastry together

WHOLEMEAL PASTRY

Follow the recipe for shortcrust pastry, using whole-meal flour instead of white flour.

FLAKY PASTRY

200 g (7 oz) plain flour
pinch of salt
150 g (5 oz) butter, or
   butter and lard mixed

about 105 ml (7 tbsp) cold
   water to mix
squeeze of lemon juice
beaten egg to glaze

Sift together the flour and salt ■ Soften the fat by 'working' it with a knife on a plate and divide it into 4 equal portions ■ Rub one-quarter of the fat into the flour and mix to a soft elastic dough with the water and lemon juice ■ On a floured board, roll the pastry to an oblong 3 times as long as it is wide ■ Put another quarter of the fat over the top two-thirds of the pastry in flakes, so that it looks like buttons on a card ■ Fold the bottom third up and the top third of the pastry down and turn it through 90° so that the folds are now at the side ■ Seal the edges of the pastry by pressing with the rolling pin. Re-roll as before and continue until all the fat is used up ■ Wrap the pastry loosely in greaseproof paper and leave it to 'rest' in the refrigerator for at least 30 minutes before using ■ Roll it out on a lightly floured board to 0.3 cm ($\frac{1}{8}$ inch) thick and use as required. Brush with beaten egg before baking to give the characteristic glaze.

Putting fat on pastry in flakes

Folding bottom third up

Sealing edges of pastry

SUETCRUST PASTRY

200 g (7 oz) self raising
 flour
5 ml (1 level tsp) salt
100 g (3½ oz) shredded
 suet

about 105–120 ml
 (7–8 tbsp) water

Mix together the flour, salt and suet. Add enough cold water to give a light, elastic dough and knead very lightly until smooth. Roll out to 0.5 cm (¼ inch) thickness ▪ This pastry may be used for both sweet and savoury dishes and can be steamed, boiled or baked; the first two are the most satisfactory methods, as baked suetcrust pastry is inclined to be hard.

MAKING A FLAN CASE

Turn the pastry on to a board and roll out to a circle about 5 cm (2 inches) wider than the flan case, ring or tin, with the rolling pin, lift the pastry and lower it into the case. Lightly press the pastry into the case then turn any surplus pastry outwards over the rim. Roll across the top with the rolling pin to trim the edges. Bake blind as described below.

Filling case with dried beans   Removing beans and paper

BAKING BLIND

Baking blind is the term used to describe cooking a pastry case or shell without a filling. To keep the case a good shape, cover the surface of the uncooked pastry with a large piece of foil or greaseproof paper, then fill with some dried beans or peas kept specially for this purpose. Bake at 200°C (400°F) mark 6 for 15 minutes. Remove the beans and paper and return the flan case to the oven for 5 minutes to allow the pastry to dry out. Remove from the oven and cool. Pastry cases which have been baked blind may be stored in a tin when cold and kept until required. Fill them with fruit or any suitable sweet or savoury mixture and garnish or decorate.

CAKES
AND BISCUITS

LINING CAKE TINS

Grease the tin by brushing with oil or melted vegetable fat. Stand the tin on a sheet of greaseproof paper and draw round it with a pencil. Cut out the shape just inside the pencilled line. Measure the depth of the tin and add an extra 5 cm (2 inches); now cut a strip of greaseproof paper this width and long enough to encircle the tin. It may be necessary to cut 2 strips to give the right length. Turn up 1 cm ($\frac{1}{2}$ inch) along one long edge of the strip and make slanting cuts at 1 cm ($\frac{1}{2}$ inch) intervals, going as far as the crease. Fit the strips neatly into place round the sides of the tin, with the snipped edge on the base. Fit the base paper into the bottom. Finally, brush all the lining paper with oil or melted fat.

With a shallow sandwich tin it is normal to line the base only, with a circle of paper that fits exactly.

Fitting paper in round tin

Fitting paper in square tin

With a rich fruit cake, double greaseproof paper should be used to prevent overbrowning and drying of the outside crust. When cooking a Christmas cake wrap an extra layer of brown or newspaper round the outside of the tin.

If you notice that a cake is browning too quickly on top, place a piece of paper over it for the second half of the cooking time.

Siliconised papers need no greasing.

Non-stick tins need no lining, as they have been specially treated. To preserve the finish, avoid using sharp knives and harsh abrasives.

VICTORIA SANDWICH

100 g (4 oz) butter or
　margarine
100 g (4 oz) caster sugar
2 eggs, beaten

100 g (4 oz) self raising
　flour, sifted
30–45 ml (2–3 tbsp) jam
caster sugar to dredge

Beating in eggs

Grease and base-line with greased greaseproof paper two 18-cm (7-inch) sandwich cake tins. Cream the fat and sugar until pale and fluffy. Beat the eggs in a little at a time, beating well after each addition ■ Lightly fold in half the flour, using a tablespoon, then fold in the rest ■ Place half the mixture in each tin and level it with a knife ■ Bake both cakes on the same shelf, at 190°C (375°F) mark 5, for about 20 minutes, or until they are well risen, golden, firm to the touch and beginning to shrink away from the sides of the tins. Turn out on to a wire rack. When cool, sandwich with jam and sprinkle the top with caster sugar.

VARIATIONS

This mixture may be varied in many ways.

Chocolate Replace 45 ml (3 level tbsp) flour with 45 ml (3 level tbsp) cocoa powder. Sandwich the cakes together with vanilla or chocolate butter cream (see page 118).

Placing mixture in tins

Orange or Lemon Add 10 ml (2 level tsp) grated orange or lemon rind to the mixture. Sandwich the cakes together with orange or lemon curd or orange or lemon butter cream. Use the juice of the fruit to make glacé icing for the top (see page 119).

Coffee Add 10 ml (2 tsp) instant coffee powder or 15 ml (1 tbsp) strong black coffee to the creamed mixture, adding it with the egg.

SWISS ROLL

2 eggs
50 g (2 oz) caster sugar
50 g (2 oz) plain flour

15 ml (1 tbsp) hot water
60 ml (4 tbsp) jam
caster sugar to dredge

Grease and line a swiss roll tin with greased greaseproof paper. Half-fill a large saucepan with water and bring to the boil; put the pan on the table on a pot stand ■ Put the eggs and the sugar into a mixing bowl and rest this on the saucepan ■ Whisk until the mixture is really stiff, pale and fluffy. Remove bowl from the pan and whisk for a further few minutes to cool the mixture ■ Sift the flour into the mixture and fold it in very lightly using a tablespoon, until all is thoroughly mixed ■ Add the water and mix in carefully with a metal spoon. Pour the mixture into the tin, spreading it out evenly with a knife.

Trimming edges of cake   Making cut at untrimmed end   Rolling sponge

Bake in the oven at 220°C (425°F) mark 7 for 7–9 minutes – the sponge is cooked when it is golden brown and feels spongy ■ Warm the jam gently in a small pan. Wring a clean tea towel out in water, spread out on a flat surface, cover with a piece of greaseproof paper and sprinkle with sugar ■ Take the cake from the oven and turn out at once on to the sugared paper ■ Using a sharp knife, trim the edges of the 2 long sides and the farther short side ■ Quickly spread the melted jam evenly on the cake to within 2.5 cm (1 inch) of the cut short edge ■ Make a cut half-way through the depth of the sponge right across the cake 2.5 cm (1 inch) from the untrimmed end. Turn the untrimmed end over, press down firmly, then roll the sponge by pulling the near end of the paper over the cake and away from yourself; roll the cake firmly ■ Leave for 5 minutes, then unwrap and put on a wire rack to cool. Dredge with sugar before serving.

CHERRY CAKE

175 g (6 oz) butter or
  margarine
175 g (6 oz) caster sugar
2 eggs, beaten
225 g (8 oz) self raising
  flour

pinch of salt
100–175 g (4–6 oz) glacé
  cherries, rinsed, well
  dried and quartered
vanilla flavouring
milk if required

Grease a loaf tin measuring about 23 × 12.5 cm (9 × 5 inches) and line with greased greaseproof paper ■ Cream the butter and sugar, then gradually beat in the eggs. Sift together the flour and salt and add the cherries ■ Fold this mixture into the creamed mixture and add a few drops of flavouring and enough milk to give a dropping consistency ■ Put into the prepared tin and bake in the oven at 180°C (350°F) mark 4 for 1¼–1½ hours, until firm to touch and golden in colour.

CHOCOLATE CAKE

75 g (3 oz) self raising flour
30 ml (2 level tbsp) ground rice
100 g (4 oz) plain chocolate, grated
100 g (4 oz) butter or margarine
75 g (3 oz) caster sugar

5–10 ml (1–2 tsp) vanilla flavouring
2 eggs, beaten
chocolate butter cream (see page 118)
chocolate glacé icing (see page 119)
crystallised violets

Grease and line with greased greaseproof paper a 15-cm (6-inch) cake tin ▪ Mix the flour and ground rice. Put the grated chocolate into a small basin, place over a saucepan of hot water and heat gently to melt the chocolate ▪ Cream the fat, sugar and flavouring until pale and fluffy. Add the melted chocolate (which should be only just warm) to the creamed mixture and mix lightly together ▪ Beat in the eggs a little at a time. Fold in the flour, put into the tin and bake in the oven at 180°C (350°F) mark 4 for 1–1¼ hours ▪ Turn out on to a wire rack to cool ▪ When cold, split in half and fill with chocolate butter cream ▪ Ice with glacé icing and decorate with crystallised violets.

GINGERBREAD

225 g (8 oz) plain flour
10–15 ml (2–3 level tsp) ground ginger
10 ml (2 level tsp) baking powder
2.5 ml (½ level tsp) bicarbonate of soda
2.5 ml (½ level tsp) salt
90 ml (6 tbsp) syrup

15 ml (1 tbsp) black treacle (optional)
75 g (3 oz) butter or margarine
100 g (4 oz) soft brown sugar
1 egg, beaten
60–150 ml (2–5 fl oz) milk

Grease and line a 20.5-cm (8-inch) square tin with greased greaseproof paper ▪ Sift the dry ingredients together. Warm the syrup, treacle (if used), fat and sugar. Make a well in the centre of the dry ingredients and add the syrup mixture. Add the egg and some of the milk, and stir well; add more milk if necessary to give a pouring consistency ▪ Pour the mixture into the tin and bake in the oven at 170°C (325°F) mark 3 for about 1 hour, until firm to the touch ▪ Cool on a wire rack, remove the paper and cut into squares.

Melting butter, sugar, syrup

Adding rolled oats

Cutting into pieces

CHOCOLATE CHIP COOKIES

Makes 20

75 g (3 oz) butter or margarine
75 g (3 oz) granulated sugar
75 g (3 oz) soft brown sugar
a few drops of vanilla flavouring

1 egg
175 g (6 oz) self raising flour
pinch of salt
50 g (2 oz) walnuts, chopped
50–100 g (2–4 oz) chocolate chips

Grease 2 baking sheets ▪ Cream the butter with the sugars and flavouring then beat in the egg. Fold in the sifted flour and salt, with the nuts and chocolate chips ▪ Drop spoonfuls of mixture on the baking sheets and bake in the oven at 180°C (350°F) mark 4 for 12–15 minutes ▪ Cool on the baking sheets for 1 minute, then place on a wire rack to finish cooling.

SHORTBREAD

Makes 8

175 g (6 oz) plain flour
a pinch of salt

125 g (4 oz) butter
50 g (2 oz) caster sugar

Crimping edges

Grease a baking sheet ▪ Sift the flour and salt together, then rub in the butter until the mixture resembles fine breadcrumbs. Add the sugar, then knead the mixture until it binds well together ▪ Turn this dough on to a lightly floured board and press into a round shape. Roll out to 1 cm ($\frac{1}{2}$ inch) thick, still keeping the round shape. Crimp the edges with the finger and thumb, mark the round into 8 sections with a knife and prick the surface with a fork ▪ Bake in the oven at 170°C (325°F) mark 3 for about 45 minutes, until firm and lightly coloured. Divide when cool.

GINGERBREAD MEN

Makes 6

175 g (6 oz) plain flour
2.5 ml (½ level tsp)
  bicarbonate of soda
5 ml (1 level tsp) ground
  ginger
50 g (2 oz) butter or
  margarine

75 g (3 oz) soft brown
  sugar
30 ml (2 tbsp) golden
  syrup
30 ml (2 tbsp) beaten egg
currants to decorate

Grease a baking sheet ▪ Sift together the dry ingredients and rub in the fat. Add the sugar and mix well ▪ Stir in the slightly warmed syrup and egg to give a pliable dough, and knead until smooth ▪ Roll out on a floured surface to 0.3 cm (⅛ inch) thickness. Cut out, using a special cutter if available, or a cardboard pattern and a sharp-pointed knife. Carefully lift the gingerbread men on to the baking sheet, keeping them well apart ▪ Give each one 3 currants for buttons and 3 more for eyes and mouth ▪ Bake in the oven at 190°C (375°F) mark 5 for 10–15 minutes, until evenly coloured. Allow to cool before removing to a wire rack.

Cutting out gingerbread men   Decorating with currants

ONE STAGE CAKES AND PASTRY

SANDWICH CAKE

100 g (4 oz) self raising
  flour
5 ml (1 level tsp) baking
  powder
100 g (4 oz) soft tub
  margarine

100 g (4 oz) caster sugar
2 eggs
jam or lemon curd to fill

Grease two 18-cm (7-inch) sandwich tins and line each base with a round of greased greaseproof paper ▪ Sift the flour and baking powder into a large bowl. Add the other ingredients, mix well, then beat for about 2 minutes. Divide evenly between the tins ▪ Bake in the oven at 180°C (350°F) mark 4 for 25–35 minutes. When cool, sandwich with jam or lemon curd ▪ For a more lavish decoration, sandwich together with butter cream and pour chocolate icing (see pages 118–119) over the top, letting it trickle down the sides.

VARIATIONS

Orange   Add the grated rind and juice of 1 orange.

Mocha   Sift 30 ml (2 level tbsp) cocoa and 15 ml (1 level tbsp) instant coffee powder with 75 g (3 oz) flour.

Chocolate, Cherry and Nut Cake   Omit 30 ml (2 level tbsp) sugar and add 25 g (1 oz) grated plain chocolate, 75 g (3 oz) chopped glacé cherries and 60 ml (4 level tbsp) chopped nuts.

Small buns   Make into 18–20 buns and bake in the oven at 200°C (400°F) mark 6 for 15–20 minutes.

FRUIT CAKE

225 g (8 oz) self raising flour
10 ml (2 level tsp) ground mixed spice
5 ml (1 level tsp) baking powder
100 g (4 oz) soft tub margarine

100 g (4 oz) soft brown sugar
225 g (8 oz) dried fruit
2 eggs
30–45 ml (2–3 tbsp) milk

Grease an 18-cm (7-inch) round cake tin and line the base with a round of greased greaseproof paper ■ Sift the flour, spice and baking powder into a large bowl, add the rest of the ingredients and mix until thoroughly combined ■ Put into the tin and bake in the oven at 170°C (325°F) mark 3 for 1¾ hours.

CHOCOLATE CAKE

175 g (6 oz) self raising flour
2.5 ml (½ level tsp) cream of tartar
2.5 ml (½ level tsp) salt
100 g (4 oz) sugar
100 g (4 oz) soft tub margarine or blended white vegetable fat

150 ml (¼ pint) milk
5 ml (1 tsp) vanilla flavouring
2 eggs
50 g (2 oz) plain chocolate, melted

Grease an 18-cm (7-inch) round cake tin ■ Sift the flour, cream of tartar and salt into a large bowl. Add the sugar, fat, milk and vanilla flavouring. Mix together then beat for 2 minutes ■ Add the eggs and chocolate and beat for 1 minute ■ Pour into the tin and bake in the oven at 180°C (350°F) mark 4 for about 1 hour 20 minutes.

TOFFEE BARS

Makes 8

100 g (4 oz) soft tub
  margarine or blended
  white vegetable fat
50 g (2 oz) sugar
50 g (2 oz) brown sugar
1.25 ml ($\frac{1}{4}$ level tsp) salt
5 ml (1 tsp) vanilla
  flavouring

1 egg
100 g (4 oz) self raising
  flour
105 ml (7 tbsp) rolled oats
50 g (2 oz) plain chocolate
50 g (2 oz) chopped nuts

Grease a 23-cm (9-inch) shallow square tin ■ Mix the fat, sugars, salt, flavouring and egg together until light and fluffy. Stir in the flour and the oats ■ Spread the mixture in the tin and bake in the oven at 180°C (350°F) mark 4 for 30 minutes ■ Melt the chocolate, spread on the cooled cake and sprinkle with nuts ■ Cut into bars.

SHORTCRUST PASTRY

100 g (4 oz) soft tub
  margarine
175 g (6 oz) plain flour,
  sifted

about 15 ml (1 tbsp) water

Place the margarine, 30 ml (2 tbsp) flour and the water in a mixing bowl. Cream it with a fork for about $\frac{1}{2}$ minute until well mixed ■ Mix in the remaining flour, to form a fairly soft dough ■ Turn it out on to a lightly floured board and knead until smooth. Roll out fairly thinly ■ This amount is enough to line a 20.5-cm (8-inch) fluted flan ring.

WHAT WENT WRONG?

RUBBED-IN AND CREAMED MIXTURES

A A cake that sinks in the middle may be due to

1 Too soft a mixture.
2 Too much raising agent.
3 Too cool an oven, which means that the centre of the cake does not rise.
4 Too hot an oven, which makes the cake appear to be done on the outside before it is cooked, so that it is taken from the oven too soon.
5 Too short a baking time.

B Close texture may be due to

1 Too much liquid.
  Too little baking powder.
  Insufficient creaming of the fat and sugar; air should be well incorporated at this stage.
4 Curdling of the creamed mixture when the eggs are added (a curdled mixture holds less air than one of the correct texture).
5 Over-stirring or beating of the flour into the creamed mixture.

C Uneven and holey texture may be caused by

1 Over-stirring or uneven mixing in of the flour.
2 Putting the mixture into the cake tin in small amounts – pockets of air are trapped in the mixture.

D Dry and crumbly texture may be due to

1 Too much baking powder.
2 Too long a cooking time in too cool an oven.

E 'Peaking' and cracking may be caused by

1 Too hot an oven.
2 The cake being placed too near the top of the oven.
3 Too stiff a mixture.
4 Too small a cake tin.

F Fruit sinking in a cake may be due to

1 Damp fruit, or sticky glacé cherries – if covered with thick syrup they should first be washed, then lightly floured.
2 Too soft a mixture – a rich fruit cake mixture should be fairly stiff, so that it can hold up the weight of the fruit.
3 Opening and banging the oven door while the cake is rising.
4 Using self raising flour where the recipe requires plain, or using too much baking powder; the cake over-rises and cannot carry the fruit with it.

G Dry fruit cakes may be due to

1 Cooking at too high a temperature.
2 Too stiff a mixture.
3 Not lining the tin thoroughly; for a large cake double greaseproof paper should be used, and a band of double brown paper should be tied round the outside of the tin to give extra protection.

H Burnt fruit on the outside of a fruit cake may be caused by

1 Too high a temperature.
2 Lack of protection – when the cake has begun to colour, cover the top with a double thickness of greaseproof or brown paper.

ICING AND DECORATING

BUTTER CREAM

100 g (4 oz) icing sugar
50 g (2 oz) butter or
  margarine

milk if required
a few drops of vanilla
  flavouring

Sift the sugar; place it with the butter in a basin and cream together with a wooden spoon until smooth, pale and of a creamy consistency — add a little milk if necessary. Beat in the vanilla flavouring ■ Or omit the vanilla flavouring and flavour the cream in any of the following ways:

Chocolate   Include 15 ml (1 level tbsp) sifted cocoa or 25 g (1 oz) melted and cooled chocolate.

Coffee   Add 10 ml (2 level tsp) instant coffee dissolved in 5 ml (1 tsp) water.

Mocha   Add 10–15 ml (2–3 tsp) sifted cocoa and 5 ml (1 tsp) instant coffee powder.

Orange or lemon   Add the grated rind of 1 orange or lemon.

Walnut   Add 25–50 g (1–2 oz) chopped walnuts and a little vanilla flavouring.

USING BUTTER CREAM

The amounts given make enough cream for one layer inside or on top of the cake. If the cake is to be both decorated all over and filled with butter cream, you will require double the quantity.

AS A FILLING

Spread the cream evenly over the lower half of the cake, taking it right to the edges, then put the top half of the cake neatly in place.

TO COVER THE CAKE

Spread the butter cream evenly all over the sides, then on the top of the cake. The sides may be rolled in chopped nuts or chocolate vermicelli. To give a more interesting effect, the surface of the butter cream can be patterned, using a fork or knife, before being decorated with crystallised fruits, nuts, glacé cherries, angelica or chocolate drops.

Another variation is to coat the sides only with butter cream and use glacé icing on the top of the cake.

GLACÉ ICING

225 g (8 oz) icing sugar, sifted   warm water to mix

Adding water gradually

Place the sugar in a basin and add the water very gradually until the icing is smooth and thick enough to coat the back of the spoon.

This basic icing may be varied as follows:

Orange or lemon   Replace the water by orange or lemon juice.

Chocolate   Sift 15 ml (1 level tbsp) cocoa with the icing sugar.

Coffee   Dissolve 10 ml (2 level tsp) instant coffee in 5 ml (1 tsp) of the water and add this when mixing the icing.

Coloured   Use food colourings to tint the icing – only a few drops are needed and they should be added when the icing is made.

USING GLACÉ ICING

The amounts given will make enough icing to cover the top of an 18-cm (7-inch) cake. The sides of the cake may be left plain or iced (in which case you will need a double quantity of icing). Alternatively, they may be brushed with melted jam and then rolled in chopped walnuts, chopped blanched almonds or lightly browned coconut. Any icing or decoration on the sides of the cake must be done before the top is iced.

To ice the top, prepare any decorations which are to be used (such as nuts, cherries, angelica, chocolate drops, crystallised fruit or silver balls, candies). Place the prepared cake on the plate on which it is to be served. Pour the icing on to the centre of the cake and spread it out evenly, stopping just inside the edges to prevent the icing from dripping down the sides. Quickly put the decorations in place before the icing sets – this holds them firmly and prevents the icing from cracking as it would do if they were added later.

Rolling cake in chopped nuts

Spreading icing evenly

ROYAL ICING

4 egg whites
900 g (2 lb) icing sugar, sifted

15 ml (1 tbsp) lemon juice
10 ml (2 tsp) glycerine

Whisk the egg whites in a bowl until slightly frothy. Stir in the sugar, a spoonful at a time with a wooden spoon. When half the sugar is incorporated, add the lemon juice ■ Continue adding more sugar, beating well after each addition until you get the right consistency – the mixture should not peak when pulled up with a wooden spoon, it should be a little stiffer for piping purposes, and thinner for flooding – Lastly, stir in the glycerine, which helps prevent the icing from becoming too hard ■ If you use an electric mixer, take care not to overbeat. It is a good idea to let it stand for 24 hours in a covered plastic container or bag before using ■ This amount is sufficient to coat the top and sides of a 23-cm (9-inch) cake. To ice the top only, use half the quantities.

TO ICE THE CAKE

Using a little icing, stick the cake firmly in the centre of a 28-cm (11-inch) cake board ■ Spoon half the icing on top of the cake; working the icing backwards and forwards with a knife to break any air bubbles, spread it over the top of the cake. Draw a clean ruler or a long palette knife across the top of the cake evenly and steadily, until the surface is smooth ■ Remove any extra icing that has been pushed to the edges. Work the rest of the icing around the sides of the cake in the same way ■ Before the icing starts to set, quickly draw it up into peaks round the sides and in a 2.5-cm (1-inch) border round the top of the cake, using a round-bladed knife. Let the icing harden for a day before adding decorations ■ If you are icing the top only, take the icing far enough down the sides to cover the almond icing completely. Rough up a 3-cm (1¼-inch) wide border round the top and the covered part of the sides ■ When the icing is set, tie a ribbon round the uncovered part of the sides.

Putting top on cake

Smoothing the join

ALMOND PASTE

350 g (12 oz) icing sugar
350 g (12 oz) ground
   almonds
1 egg, beaten

5 ml (1 tsp) almond
   flavouring
juice of ½ a lemon

Sift the sugar and stir in the almonds. Add the beaten egg and almond flavouring and gradually stir in the dry ingredients, adding enough of the lemon juice to form a stiff dough. Form into a ball and knead lightly to remove any cracks ■ This amount is sufficient to cover the top and sides of a 23-cm (9-inch) cake. If you intend to decorate the top only of the cake, make up half the amount. Cut off and reserve a small piece if you want to make almond paste decorations.

TO ALMOND-ICE THE CAKE

Trim the top of the cake to make it completely level. Measure round it, using a piece of string ■ Sieve 225 g (8 oz) apricot jam and brush it generously round the sides of the cake ■ Cut the almond paste in half. Halve one portion again and form each quarter-portion into a sausage-shape; roll out each of these half as long as the piece of string and as wide as the cake is deep ■ Press the strips firmly on to the sides of the cake, smooth the joins with a knife and square the edges ■ Roll the cake edgewise on the table or board to get a flat finish ■ Brush the top of the cake and the top edge of the almond paste with jam ■ Dredge the table top or board heavily with icing sugar, then roll out the remaining paste to a round to fit the top of the cake ■ Put the cake upside-down, exactly in the centre of the almond paste, press down firmly and smooth the join ■ Turn the cake the right way up and leave for at least 24 hours before icing – preferably for 6–7 days.

Smoothing icing

Smoothing icing on side

Squaring edges

ALMOND PASTE DECORATIONS

Decorations for a Christmas cake can be made very easily from almond paste. Choose a design with a simple, fairly bold outline – stars, candles, Christmas trees, holly leaves – draw it on stiff paper and cut out the pattern. Some parts of the design may look more attractive if carried out in a second colour, eg the tub of a Christmas tree or the flame of a candle, but do not use more than two colours, or the design will look too fussy. Cut off the portion of the paper pattern that is to be made in the second colour.

Add a little edible colouring to a piece of the almond paste, kneading it in until the colour is even. Sprinkle the working surface with a little icing sugar and roll out the almond paste very thinly. Put on it the pattern pieces that are to be made in that particular colour and cut round them with a sharp-pointed knife. (Do not press too firmly on the almond paste or finger marks will show.) Remove the patterns, neaten up the edges of the paste pieces if necessary and use the pointed knife to mark in any veins, branches, etc. Cut out the remaining shapes from a piece of almond paste tinted with the second colour. For holly berries make tiny balls of red paste. Leave the shapes on a plate until quite dry – 2–3 days if possible – or they will mark the royal icing. Lay any leaves over a twist of greaseproof paper to give them a lifelike curve.

Draw a circle on a piece of paper the size of the cake top and arrange the almond paste pieces on it in the chosen pattern. Then, using a pair of tweezers, lift each piece into the same position on the cake top and stick it with a tiny spot of icing. A birthday cake may be decorated in a similar way; for a child, use nursery rhyme or toy cut-outs.

BREADS AND SCONES

QUICK ROLLS

Makes 9

225 g (8 oz) plain flour
10 ml (2 level tsp) baking
    powder
5 ml (1 level tsp) salt

25 g (1 oz) butter or
    margarine
about 150 ml (¼ pint) milk

Sieve the dry ingredients into a bowl. Rub in the fat until the mixture resembles fine breadcrumbs ▪ Make a well in the centre, add the milk and mix together with a round-bladed knife to give a fairly soft dough ▪ Draw it together with the finger-tips and turn it on to a lightly floured board ▪ Divide into 9 portions and shape into round rolls. Place on a greased and floured baking sheet, brush with milk and bake in the oven at 220°C (425°F) mark 7 for 15–20 minutes ▪ Eat these rolls while they are still fresh.

QUICK WHITE LOAF

Makes 2 loaves

15 g (½ oz) fresh yeast or
    7.5 ml (1½ level tsp)
    dried yeast and a pinch
    of sugar
about 300 ml (½ pint)
    tepid water

450 g (1 lb) strong plain
    flour
5 ml (1 level tsp) salt

Grease 2 baking sheets ▪ If using dried yeast, dissolve the sugar in the water, sprinkle in the yeast and leave for 10–15 minutes until frothy ▪ Mix the flour and salt in a bowl, make a well in the centre and add the yeast liquid. Mix to an elastic dough, adding more liquid if necessary. Turn on to a lightly floured surface and knead for about 5 minutes, until really smooth. Divide the dough into 2 portions then knead each into a round ▪ Place on a baking sheet and cover with a clean tea towel. Leave to rise in a warm place for about 30–45 minutes until doubled in size and springing back when lightly pressed ▪ Bake in the oven at 230°C (450°F) mark 8 for about 30 minutes until well risen and golden brown and sounding hollow when the bottom is tapped. Cool on a wire rack.

QUICK WHOLEMEAL LOAVES

Makes 2 loaves

15 ml (3 level tsp) sugar
about 450 ml (¾ pint)
  water
15 ml (1 level tbsp) dried
  yeast

350 g (12 oz) wholemeal
  flour
350 g (12 oz) strong white
  flour
15 ml (3 level tsp) salt

Grease 2 baking sheets ■ Dissolve 5 ml (1 tsp) sugar in a cupful of warm water (taken from the measured amount), then sprinkle the dried yeast on the top; leave until frothy (10–15 minutes) ■ Add with the rest of the liquid to the dry ingredients and mix to a soft, scone-like dough. Divide the dough into 2 portions, shape into rounds and flatten the tops ■ Place on a baking sheet, and cover with a clean dry tea towel. Leave to rise in a warm place until the dough is doubled in size and will spring back when lightly pressed with a floured finger ■ Bake in the oven at 220°C (425°F) mark 7 for about 30 minutes, or until the loaves are firm to the touch and sound hollow when tapped underneath.

Adding yeast to flour

Covering dough

Loaves sliced

OVEN SCONES

Makes 10–12

225 g (8 oz) self-raising
  flour
1.25 ml (¼ level tsp) salt
50 g (2 oz) butter or
  margarine

25 g (1 oz) sugar
50 g (2 oz) currants
about 150 ml (¼ pint) milk

Stirring in sugar and currants

Rolling out dough

Brushing tops with milk

Grease a baking sheet ■ Sift the flour and salt into a bowl. Cut the fat into it and rub in until the mixture resembles fine breadcrumbs ■ Stir in the sugar and currants. Add the milk to give a fairly soft dough. Draw the mixture together with the finger-tips and turn on to a very lightly floured board; form into a flat round and roll out 2.5 cm (1 inch) thick ■ Cut into rounds with a 5-cm (2-inch) cutter and place on the greased baking sheet. Brush the tops with milk and cook in the oven at 220°C (425°F) mark 7 for about 10 minutes until golden brown ■ Remove to a cooling rack and leave till cold ■ Serve split in half and buttered.

DROP SCONES OR SCOTCH PANCAKES

Makes 15–18

125 g (4 oz) self raising flour	1 egg
30 ml (2 level tbsp) sugar	150 ml (¼ pint) milk

These scones may be cooked on a special 'girdle', in a heavy frying pan or on a solid hot-plate. Season the surface by rubbing with salt on a pad of kitchen paper; wipe clean and grease the surface very lightly ■ Put the flour and sugar in a bowl, break in the egg, add half the milk and beat until smooth. Add the rest of the milk and beat until bubbles rise to the surface ■ Heat the girdle, pan or hot-plate until the fat is hazing. Wipe the surface with a piece of kitchen paper, spoon on the batter and cook on one side ■ When bubbles appear on the surface of the scone, turn it over with a palette knife and cook for another ½–1 minute, or until golden brown ■ Remove and place on a wire rack. Cover with a clean tea cloth while the rest are being cooked ■ Serve buttered or with whipped cream and jam.

Spooning on the batter

Turning over pancakes

INDEX

Almond Paste, 121–2
Apple
  and Blackberry Charlotte, 90
  Cake, 112
  Muesli, 12
  Pie, 86–7
  Sauce, 102
  Stuffed Baked, 85
Apricot Fool (with variations), 91
Aubergines, Stuffed, 72
Avocados, Dressed, 24

Bacon, 15, 40–41
  Fried, 15
  Grilled, 15
  Liver, and Mushrooms, 54
  to bake, 41
  to boil, 41
Baked
  Apples, Stuffed, 85
  Eggs, 75
  Jacket Potatoes, 60
  Jam Sponge, 87
  Kippers, 16
  Mushrooms, 64
  Plaice with Mushrooms, 29
Bananas with Honey and Orange,
  87
Barbecue Sauce, 100
Barbecued Spare Ribs, 53
Beans, 63, 64
Beef, 33–4
  accompaniments for, 34
  Casserole, 48
  Chilli Con Carne, 49
  Cottage Pie, 50
  Curried, 49
  Goulash, 50
  Hamburgers, 46
  Steak and Kidney Pudding, 48
  Steak and Mushroom Pie, 47
  to carve, 44
Beetroots, 66
Biscuits
  Chocolate Chip Cookies, 113
  Gingerbread Men, 114
  Shortbread, 113
  Syrup Flapjacks, 112
Blackberry and Apple Charlotte, 90
Blue Cheese Dip, 25
Boiled Potatoes, 59
  Rice, 79
Brandy Butter, 101
Bread Sauce, 99
Breakfast, 11–19
  Bacon, 15
  Cereals, 12–13
  Coffee, 17–19
  Eggs, 13–14
  Fruits and juices, 11–12

Kippers, 16
Sausages, 14
Tea, 19
Broad Beans, 64
Brussels Sprouts, 61
Butter
  Brandy, 101
  Cream, use and variations, 118

Cabbage, 62
Cakes, 107–25
  Apple, 112
  Cherry, 109
  Chocolate, 110, (one stage) 115
  Christmas, 111
  faults in making, 116–17
  Fruit, 112, (one stage) 115
  Gingerbread, 110
  Sandwich, (one stage) 114–15,
    variations of, 115
  Swiss Roll, 108–9
  tins, to line, 107
  Toffee Bars (one stage), 116
  to ice, 120, 121–2
  Victoria Sandwich, with
    variations, 108
Cakes and Pastry (one stage), 114–16
Cannelloni, 81
Caramel, Crème, 96
Carrots, 65
Carving, meat, 44–6
Casserole
  Beef, 48
  of Chicken, 58
Cauliflower, 63
Celery, 66
Cereals, 12–13
Charlotte, Apple and Blackberry,
  90–91
Cheese
  Blue Cheese Dip, 25
  Cheesey Grilled Cod, 32
  Courgette and Cheese Flan, 74
  Macaroni, 83
  Omelette, 76
  on Toast, 74–5
  Quiche Lorraine, 75
Cheesecake, Lemon, 93
Cherry Cake, 109
Chicken
  Casserole of, 58
  Coronation, 57
  Creamy, and Tarragon Pie, 58
  Curried, 49
  Liver Pâté, 23
  Livers on Toast, 71
  Risotto, 79
  Roast, 56
  Soup, 23
  Stock, 20

Chilli Con Carne, 49
Chipped Potatoes, 60
Chocolate
  Cake, 110, (one stage) 115
  Chip Cookies, 113
  Mousse, 92
Christmas Cake, 111
  Pudding, 88–9
Cod, 27, 30
  Cheesey Grilled, 32
Coffee, and making of, 17–19
Coleslaw, 69
Cookies, Chocolate Chip, 113
Cooking Equipment, 8–9
Corn on the Cob, 24–5
Coronation Chicken, 57
Cottage Pie, 50
Courgettes, 63
  and Cheese Flan, 74
Cream
  Butter (and variations), 118
  Ice, 97
Creamed Potatoes, 60
Creamy Chicken and Tarragon Pie,
  58
Crème Caramel, 96
Cress, 67
Croutons, 22
Crumble, Rhubarb, 85
Cucumber, 67
Curried Beef, 49
Curry, 49

Dip, Blue Cheese, 25
Dressing, French, 68
Dried Fruit with Yogurt, 12
Drop Scones, 125
Dutch Cabbage, 62

Eggs, 13–14
  à la Mornay, 77
  Baked, 75
  Boiled, 13
  Curried, 49
  Custard Sauce, 101
  Florentine, 77
  Fried, 14, 15
  Mayonnaise, 78
  Omelette, 76
  Poached, 13
  Scotch, 76–7
  Scrambled, 14
Equipment, Cooking, 8–9

Fish, 27–32
  Baked Plaice with Mushrooms,
    29
  Cheesey Grilled Cod, 32
  Curried, 49
  Fried Plaice Fillets, 29

Fish (cont.)
  Herrings in Oatmeal, 31
  in Batter, 30
  Kedgeree, 32
  Kippers, 16
  Mackerel Pâté, 24
  Pie, 31
  Poached Smoked Haddock, 31
  types of, 27–8
Flaky Pastry, 105
Flans
  case, to make, 106
  Courgette and Cheese, 74
  Fruit, 92–3
Flapjacks, Syrup, 112
Florentine Eggs, 75
Florida Cocktail, 25
Fool, Apricot (and variations), 91
Forcemeat, 102
French
  Beans, 63
  Dressing, 68
  Onion Soup, 21
Fried
  Bacon, 15
  Bread, 14, 15
  Kippers, 16
  Plaice Fillets, 29
  Sausages, 14
Fruit
  Breakfast, 11–12
  Cake, 112, (one stage) 115
  Dried, with Yogurt, 12
  Flans, 92–3
  Fool, 91
  Juices, 11
  Salad, 96
  Sorbet, 95
  Summer Pudding, 94
  Trifle, 92
  Water Ices, 95

Gammon, 40, 41
Gingerbread, 110
  Men, 114
Glacé Icing (and variations), 119
Goulash, 50
Grapefruit, 12
  Florida Cocktail, 25
Gravy, 100
Green Salad, 69
Greens, Spring, 61
Grilled
  Kippers, 16
  Mackerel, 30
  Mushrooms, 64
  Pork Chops with Apple Rings, 54
  Sausages, 14
  Steak, 46

Haddock, 27, 31, 32
  Smoked, Poached, 32
Ham and Leeks au Gratin, 73
Hamburgers, 46
Herbs, 68, 76
Herrings, 28
  in Oatmeal, 31
Hotpot, Pork and Prune, 53

Ice Cream (and variations), 97
Icing, Cake, 118–22
  Almond Paste (and decorations), 121
  Butter (and variations), 118
  Glacé (and variations), 119
  Royal, 120
Imperial measure, converting to metric, 7
Irish Stew, 81

Jacket Baked Potatoes, 60
Jam Sponge, Baked, 87
Juices, fruit, 11

Kebabs, Lamb, 51
Kedgeree, 32
Kidneys, 16
  Grilled, 54
Kippers, 16, 28
  Baked, 16
  Fried, 16
  Grilled, 16

Lamb, 34–6
  accompaniments for, 36
  Irish Stew, 51
  Kebabs, 51
  Liver, Bacon and Mushrooms, 54
  Moussaka, 52
  Navarin of, 52
  to carve, 44–5
Lasagne, 80
  Al Forno, 84
Leeks, 65
  and Ham au Gratin, 73
Lemon
  Cheesecake, 93
  Meringue Pie, 88
Lettuce, 67
Liver
  Bacon and Mushrooms, 54
  Chicken, on Toast, 71
  Chicken, Pâté, 23
  Loaf, Quick White, 123
Loaves, Quick Wholemeal, 124

Macaroni, 80
  Cheese, 83
Mackerel, 28
  Grilled, 30
  Pâté, 24
  Marinade, 51
Marrow
  Stuffed, 71
  Vegetable, 62
Mashed Potatoes, 59
Mayonnaise, 68–9
  Egg, 78
Measuring, 7–8
  conversion table, Imperial to metric, 7
  equivalent measures, 8
Meat, 33–54
  Bacon and Gammon, 40–41
  Beef, 33–4
  carving, 44–6
  Forcemeat for, 102

Lamb, 34–6
Pork, 37–9
Steak, 34
Metric measures, converting to Imperial, 7, 8
Mince Pies, 90
Minestrone Soup, 22
Mint, 68
  Sauce, 99
Moussaka, 52
Mousse
  Chocolate, 92
  Raspberry, 91
Muesli, Apple, 12
Mushrooms, 14, 64
  Baked, 64
  for Salads, 64
  Grilled, 64
  Omelette, 76
  on Toast, 71
  Sauté, 64

Navarin of Lamb, 52

Oatmeal, Herrings in, 31
Omelette, and fillings, 76
One Stage Cakes and Pastry, 114–16
Onion, 67
  and Sage Stuffing, 102
  French, Soup, 21
  with White or Cheese Sauce, 67
Orange
  Florida Cocktail, 25
  for Breakfast, 11
  Salad, 69
  Water Ice, 95
Oven
  Scones, 124–5
  thermostat settings (conversion table), 7
  use of, 6–7

Pancakes, 86
  Savoury, 78
  Scotch, 125
Parsley, 68, 98
Parsnips, 65
Pasta, 80–84
  Niçoise, 82
Pastry, 104–6
  baking blind, 106
  Flaky, 105
  Flan case, to make, 106
  making, 104
  Shortcrust, 104, (one stage) 116
  Suetcrust, 106
  Wholemeal, 105
Pastry and cakes (one stage), 114–16
Pâté, 23–4
  Chicken Liver, 23
  Mackerel, 24
Peas, 64
Peppers, Stuffed, 80
Pies
  Apple, 86–7
  Cottage, 50
  Creamy Chicken and Tarragon, 58

Pies (cont.)
  Fish, 31
  Lemon Meringue, 88
  Mince, 90
  Steak and Mushroom, 47
Pizza, Quick, 73
Plaice, 28
  Baked with Mushrooms, 29
  Fried, Fillets, 29
Plums, Stewed, 89
Poached Smoked Haddock, 31
Popovers, 103
Pork, 36–9
  accompaniments for, 102
  and Prune Hot Pot, 53
  Barbecued Spare Ribs, 53
  Chops, Grilled with Apple Rings, 54
  to carve, 45–6
Porridge, 13
Potatoes, 59–61
  Baked in their Jackets, 60
  Boiled, 59
  Chipped, 60
  Creamed, 60
  Mashed, 59
  Roast, 60
  Salad, 70
  Sauté, 61
Prune and Pork Hotpot, 53
Pudding
  Steak and Kidney, 48
  Yorkshire, 103
Puddings, Cold, 91–7
  Apricot Fool, 91
  Chocolate Mousse, 93
  Crème Caramel, 96
  Fruit Flans, 92–3
    Salad, 96
    Sorbet, 95
    Trifle, 93
  Ice Cream, 97
  Lemon Cheesecake, 93
  Orange Water Ice, 95
  Raspberry Mousse, 91
  Strawberry Shortcake, 94–5
  Summer, 94
Puddings, Hot, 85–90
  Apple Pie, 86–7
  and Blackberry Charlotte, 90
  Baked Jam Sponge, 87
  Bananas with Honey and Orange, 87
  Christmas Pudding, 88–9
  Lemon Meringue Pie, 88
  Mince Pies, 90
  Pancakes, 86
  Rhubarb Crumble, 85
  Stewed Plums, 89
  Stuffed Baked Apples, 85

Quiche Lorraine, 75
Quick
  Pizza, 73
  Rolls, 123
  White Loaf, 123
  Wholemeal Loaves, 124

Radishes, 68
Raspberry, 11, 91
  Mousse, 91
Recipe, working from, 6
Rhubarb Crumble, 85
Rice, 79–80
  Boiled, 79
  Chicken Risotto, 79
  Stuffed Peppers, 80
Risotto, Chicken, 79
Roast
  Chicken, 56
  Potatoes, 60–61
  Turkey, 55
Rolls
  Quick, 123
  Sausage, 72
Royal Icing, 120
Runner Beans, 63

Salads, 69–70
  Coleslaw, 69
  French Dressing, 68
  Fruit, 96
  Green, 69
  Orange, 69
  Potato, 70
  Tomato, 70
  Winter, 70
Sandwich Cake (one stage, with variations), 114–15
Sauces, Savoury and Sweet, 98–103
Sausage
  Fried, 14
  Grilled, 14
  Rolls, 72
  Stuffing, 102
Sauté
  Mushrooms, 64
  Potatoes, 61
Savoury Pancakes, 78
Savoy Cabbage, 62
Scones
  Drop, 125
  Oven, 124–5
Scotch
  Eggs, 75–7
  Pancakes, 125
Shortbread, 113
Shortcake, Strawberry, 94–5
Shortcrust Pastry, 104, (one stage) 116
Smoked
  Cod, 27
  Haddock, 27
  Kedgeree, 32
  Poached Haddock, 31
Snacks and Suppers, 71–8
Sorbet, Fruit, 95
Soup, 20–23
  Chicken, 23
  Cream of Mushroom, 22
  croutons for, 22
  French Onion, 21
  Minestrone, 22
  Tomato, 21
  Watercress, 23

Spaghetti, 80
  Alla Carbonara, 82–3
  Bolognese, 82
Spare Ribs, Barbecued, 53
Spinach, 62
  Eggs Florentine, 75
Sponge, Jam, Baked, 87
Spring Greens, 61
Sprouts, Brussels, 61
Starters, 23–5
Steak, 34
  and Kidney Pudding, 48
  and Mushroom Pie, 47
  Goulash, 50
  Grilled, 47
Stew, Irish, 51
Stewed Plums, 89
Stocks, 20
Strawberry Shortcake, 94–5
Stuffed
  Aubergines, 72
  Baked Apples, 85
  Marrow, 71
  Peppers, 80
Stuffing, 102
  Forcemeat, 102
  Sage and Onion, 102
  Sausage, 102
Suetcrust Pastry, 106
Summer Pudding (and variations), 94
Suppers and Snacks, 71–8
Swedes, 65
Swiss Roll, 108–9
Syrup Flapjacks, 112

Tarragon and Creamy Chicken Pie, 58
Tea, making of, 19
Temperature, oven tables, 7
Toast, Cheese on, 74–5
Toffee Bars (one stage), 116
Tomatoes, 11, 14, 76
  Baked, 66
  Grilled, 66
  Salad, 70
  Sauce, 99, 101
  Soup, 21
Trifle, Fruit, 92
Turkey, 102
  Roast, 55
  Strogonoff, 56
Turnips, 64

Vegetable Marrow, 62
Vegetables and Salads, 59–70
Victoria Sandwich, with variations, 108

Watercress, 67
Water Ice, Orange, 95
White Sauce, and variations, 98–9
Wholemeal Pastry, 105
  Quick Loaves, 124
Winter Salad, 70

Yogurt with Dried Fruit, 12
Yorkshire Pudding, 34, 103